D0269563

HOW TO
Break
90
AT THE WEEKEND

Today's Golfer

ISBN 0-9533087-8-2

Published by
Emap Active
Bretton Court
Bretton
Peterborough PE3 8DZ

Produced by
Publishing Promotions
1 High Street
Princes Risborough
Bucks HP27 0AG

INTRODUCTION

Let's face it, we could all improve our game — few golfers are complete all-rounders, and even the Pros need to practice often. For those of us who get to play mainly at weekends, our aim may be just to play a good round that lets us hold up our heads at the 19th hole!
There are many aspects of golf that need sorting out, and these are what this book is about. Poor ball flight, bad posture, bunker traps — these and many other difficulties should all be problems of the past when you have read these pages. Now go on to Beat 90...

CONTENTS

Key thoughts   4
Match–winning techniques from the experts

Winning ways   16
Two dozen tips towards a better game

How do I play this?   22
Reading the shots in difficult conditions

Ten ways to cure that slice   28
How to say goodbye to the dreaded banana shot

The power issue   38
Add those vital extra yards to your drive

Short game shots   46
Improve your performance around the greens

More birdies, fewer bogies   52
Start marking birdies on your scorecard

Be a better putter   60
Hole more long putts and impress your friends

The best bunker tips ever   66
How to get out of every bunker you come across

Save shots before you play   72
Try a warm–up routine for a better game

Quick fixes   78
Tips that will help improve your score

Buyer's guide   86
How to go shopping for the best golf gear

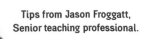

Tips from Jason Froggatt,
Senior teaching professional.

KEY THOUGHTS

Try this range of techniques to improve your next game of golf.

DOES THE HUNCHBACK RING ANY BELLS?

Inconsistent and poor ball flight generally comes from a poor line of swing caused by bad posture. Take a close look at these two pictures and you can easily spot the difference between a good-looking athletic set-up (above right) and the all-too-familiar hunched address position (above left) shared by so many poor players.

GETTING SET

Correct posture, no matter what size or shape you are, is achieved with this three-step move.

1 The first step to finding good posture is to stand with your chin off your chest, holding a club in front of you with the shaft parallel to the ground and creating a 90 degree angle between the shaft and your spine.

2 Then bend from the hips until the clubhead touches the ground, making sure you maintain the angle between the shaft and spine.

The spine angle is fixed by bending from the hips.

The chin is held off the chest.

Grip the club firmly but without tension.

The distance between feet and clubhead is determined by posture.

3 Now slightly flex the knees... and you're there. Keep practising the exercise until this posture feels completely natural.

"It's so important to establish the right grip. Then all you need is good rhythm"

LONG PUTT TIP

The secret of success on long putts is to make sure your backswing (picture 1 above) and throughswing (picture 2 below) are of equal length. The stroke should be smooth, and the clubhead should accelerate slightly through the ball.

Once you've got the ball inside the circle, all that's left is a simple tap-in.

RING OF CONFIDENCE

Here's a simple practice drill to rid yourself of one of the most common curses to afflict high handicappers, three-putting. Use string and tee pegs to create a circle a yard around the hole and then concentrate on getting balls into that circle from 30 feet and beyond. When the ball is in the circle, your worries are over — all that's left is a simple tap-in.

GET A GRIP

Do you have problems with your grip? If you have yet to break 90 on the course, then the answer is almost certainly yes. Check by looking at the clubhead when your hands are at waist height in the backswing. If the toe is pointing to the sky, you are OK. But if the face points to the ground you have all sorts of problems — you will deloft the clubface at impact and either hook or pull the ball. Looking down on your hands at address, you should see two or two-and-a-half knuckles on your left hand. The vees formed between the thumb and forefinger on each hand should not point outside the right shoulder.

With a grip like this, you are going to hook the shot.

If the club is pointing down, start shouting Fore!

Count your knuckles. You should be able to see two of them.

The toe of the club should point upwards.

"If you've still to break 90, chances are that you're gripping the club wrongly"

"The cause of poor putting is often found in the wrists"

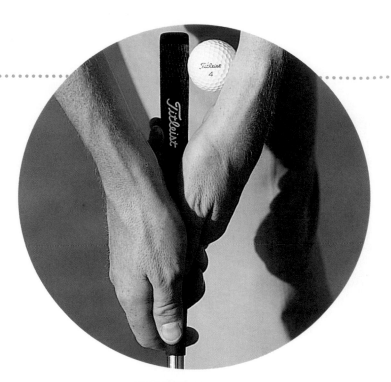

HOW TO AVOID A PUTTING BREAKDOWN

One of the most common faults I see with poor putters is inconsistent contact at impact, generally caused by the breakdown of the left wrist. I recommend the following simple drill to help stabilise the wrist throughout the stroke.

PRACTICE PUTTING DRILL

Place a ball on the ground, grip a little further down the handle of the putter than normal with the left hand and lodge another ball between the handle and your left wrist (picture 1 above). Add your right hand and set up to the ball on the ground. You might have to bend your knees a little more than normal as a result of gripping further down the handle. Now make the stroke. Any breaking down of the wrists will result in the upper ball dropping to the ground (picture 2). Once you can putt repeatedly without causing the ball to drop, you've cracked it. Take the lodged ball away and continue with the same action.

HOW TO HIT THE BALL FROM ABOVE YOUR FEET

Anyone aspiring to play the game to a good standard needs the knowledge and ability to hit the ball off any type of lie. One of the more difficult tests is where the ball has to be played from above your feet. This is how it's done.

"Players cannot expect to achieve low handicaps unless they can cope with all lies"

1 The first thing to acknowledge is that the flight of the ball from this lie (picture 1 above) will naturally be from right to left. So allow for it when you take aim Now adopt a tension-free address position, with the weight towards the balls of the feet as much as the lie will reasonably permit, and the ball in the centre of your stance. Bad balance and tension lead to either rocking back and thinning the ball or leaning too far forward and striking the turf before it. Because the slope has the effect of bringing the ball closer to you, grip the club further down the handle than normal. You are now in the correct position to play the shot.

2 This picture shows how the backswing is mainly body dominated, with the hands and arms naturally travelling around it on a flatter plane. On the downswing and through impact, keep up a smooth tempo and good balance. Don't make the mistake of 'pulling out' of the shot by ensuring you fully transfer your weight to the front foot.

Tips from Simon Wordsworth, Head teaching professional.

"The breakdown of the relationship between arms and body is one of the prime reasons for bad pitching"

HOW TO PITCH THE BALL CLOSE

Good and consistent pitching from 50 yards of the flag is achieved by making sure the arms and body work together at similar speeds and stay attached throughout.

Here's a great drill to give you that essential feeling of 'togetherness'. I guarantee that it will work wonders for your pitching. Position the ball in the centre of your stance and concentrate 60 percent of your weight on your left side. Now place a headcover under each armpit, keeping your arms tucked in just enough to keep the covers in place. Keep your weight on the left side, swing away and then through the ball, making sure the headcovers do not drop to the floor. The limitation on this drill is left arm parallel to the ground on the backswing and right arm parallel to the ground on the through–swing, probably equating to a maximum shot of about 50 yards. Any breakdown of the desired relationship between the arms and body will result in either one or both headcovers falling to the ground.

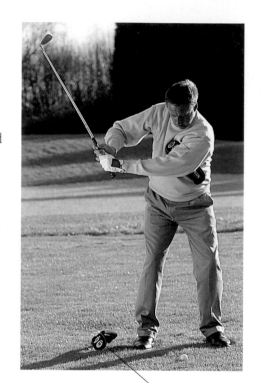

The headcover falls as the arm separates from the body...

...but not when arms and body remain together.

At address, tuck your arms in with just enough pressure to keep the headcovers in place.

The same applies on the through–swing. When the headcovers drop you lose control of your pitch shot.

JUST DON'T MOVE:

A common fault is having too many moving parts during the putting stroke. The head moves, the shoulders turn, the arms lift... and the knees often join in as well! Because you don't need power, you don't need movement. All it will do is complicate what should be a simple stroke.

"Keep your body still on the putting green to get a better roll"

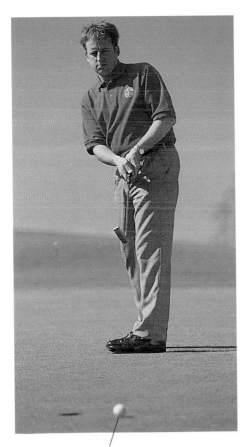

Too many moving parts means you miss. It's that simple.

The shoulders tilt — they do not turn.

Simply swivel your head to watch the putt and maintain the angle of the spine. Do not look up.

The knees should remain perfectly still and, as a result, so do the hips.

The putterface 'looks at' the hole and is still low to the ground after impact.

Tips from Derek Simpson,
Senior teaching professional.

HOW TO HIT A DRAW

Here I am on the tee of one of the best-known holes in Britain – the 18th on the Brabazon course at The Belfry. To ensure I get within comfortable distance to hit the green in two, I need to hit the ball over the water with draw spin (right to left). All the work to achieve success is done before I actually move the clubhead away from the ball at address. Here's how I would play the shot.

"Knowing how to shape a ball is a must if you want to progress at the game"

1 I put the ball on a tee and then walk to the back of the teeing ground so I can get a good mental image and a feel for the shot I want to play.

Before attempting this shot on the course, it is best to go to the practice ground and discover for yourself exactly the relationship you achieve between set-up and ball flight. You will then know the exact set-up for differing amounts of required draw.

2 I make my way back to the ball and ensure it sits high on the tee, at least half the height again of the clubface of my driver. This helps promote a draw flight pattern.

3 Using my normal grip, I aim the clubhead at where I want the ball to land and adopt a stance with my feet, knees, hips and shoulders all slightly closed (right) of the target. This will result in the club moving slightly on the inside at takeaway and an in-to-out path at impact to provide the necessary draw spin, which, incidentally, will also help to put extra run on the ball.

HOW TO GET ON THE RIGHT PLANE

Practising on a slope with the ball below the level of the feet is an excellent way to help the many players whose swings are too flat.Taking the club back on a flat plane positions the right elbow too low in the backswing, and by the time the clubhead reaches the top it points well left of target. From there, the most common way of getting the club back to the ball is by coming 'over the top' on an out-to-in path through the hitting area, usually causing a slice.

"Swing plane dictates shape"

1

2

STOP YOUR 'FLAT' SWING

Having the ball below the level of the feet (picture 1 left) demands a more upright swing and positions the club where it should be at the top, with the head pointing parallel to the target line. The butt end also points at the ball rather than well outside it.

Spend time practising (picture 2 right) and, once you have acquired a feeling for the correct plane, adopt it into your regular game.

Locking the right knee usually results in an over-the-top action and a slice.

"A locked knee in the backswing can lead to all sorts of problems"

Retaining the basket in position means the body is turning correctly and will result in improved consistency and power.

Keeping the right leg flexed enables the hips to turn correctly in the backswing rather than lift.

UNLOCK YOUR PROBLEM

A common mistake I see being made by many players is the locking of the right knee during the backswing, causing the right hip to lift rather than turn and the elbows to separate. The outcome is nearly always an 'over-the-top' action of the shoulders from the top of the swing... and a slice. A drill I recommend to solve the problem is to place between the thighs a small ball basket. Gently squeeze to keep it in place and then make a swing. Any locking of the right knee will lead to the basket dropping to the ground. Keeping it in position means you are turning correctly.

A Break 90 tip from Alastair Davies, Teaching professional.

HOW TO FADE AWAY

Playing the deliberate fade, where the ball sets out left of target and cuts back to it towards the end of its flight, is a useful shot to have in your armoury. Not only does it allow you to play away from and around trouble, but it also gives a softer ball landing when required.

'Shaping the flight of the ball is usually fixed at address'

1 Most of the work in achieving the fade is completed at address. The feet, hips and shoulders are all aimed to the left of the target and the clubhead is swivelled in the hands clockwise until it faces directly at where you want the ball to go.

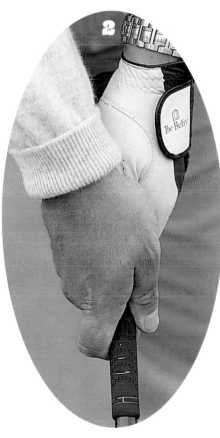

2 In swivelling the club, don't be afraid to allow the hands to move a little further to the left on the grip than normal and into what is called the weak position.

3 Now simply swing the club along your feet, hips and body line, causing the clubface to cut across the ball on an out-to-in path and imparting slice spin (left to right) on the ball. The amount of spin will depend on exactly how far left you are aligned. The more you practise, the more control you will have over the amount of fade.

WINNING WAYS

Two dozen tips towards that better game

2 LOW AND SLOW START

Many golf swings are ruined almost before they begin because the club is picked up with the hands instead of being moved away low and slow by the hands, arms and shoulders acting together. A good practice drill to get on the right track is to position a ball about 12 to 15 inches behind your right foot and make sure the clubhead passes over it on its way back.

1 DOUBLE BONUS

Several products have been marketed to help players develop good rhythm and tempo. But one of the most successful aids is to simply swing a couple of irons together. Their combined weight makes it virtually impossible to swing too quickly and you will soon discover how a proper action should feel.

IMPROVE YOUR TEMPO

3 LET ERNIE HELP YOU

One of the best ways of establishing a smooth and repeating tempo is to mentally count 'one and two' or say a couple of words to yourself during the swing. Ernie Els has one of the most rhythmic swings in the game so try matching your tempo by slowly saying 'Ernie' in your backswing and 'Els' in your downswing.

4 TOP ADVICE

Many swings fall apart from the top of the backswing because players throw their bodies at the ball with a wild lunge. Any chances of a smooth and accelerating action through the ball disappear. Concentrate at the top of the swing on pulling the hands and club down and through the impact area. You'll be surprised by the result.

5 LET IT RUN

The chip and run shot is ideal when there's a slight bank leading up to the green. Stand with the ball towards your back foot and your body square to the flag. Push your knees forward towards the target. With your hands positioned at the bottom of the grip, this becomes a fairly stiff wristed shot. After a short backswing pull the club through the ball, hitting it slightly on the downswing. Do not follow through very far.

6 PERFECTING THE LOB SHOT

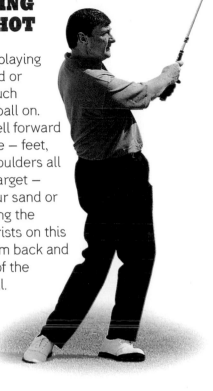

A great shot when playing over a water hazard or bunker with not much green to pitch the ball on. Position the ball well forward in your open stance — feet, knees, hips and shoulders all aiming left of the target — with the face of your sand or lob wedge still facing the target. Use your wrists on this shot. Just cock them back and then pull the butt of the club across the ball. You'll get a very lofted shot and the ball will come down very softly.

SAVE SHOTS

7 PUTT WITH A 7-IRON

You don't always have to be on the green to putt. In fact you don't always need a putter in your hand to putt. Choose an iron which will pitch the ball about two to three feet on the green and then run the rest of the distance. The only reason you are not using your putter from just off the green is because of the slight rough on the fringe which you need to carry. Using a 7-iron you simply hit the ball at the same pace as if you were using your putter.

8 ROLL OUT THE SAND

There are occasions when you need the ball to roll after you've played a bunker shot. It may be when the ball is sitting down slightly or the pin could be at the back of the green. Stand slightly squarer to the target line than normal and close the clubface just a little bit. Try to hit more sand than normal onto the green. The ball will then pitch and run up to the flag

9 LOOSEN UP

Everyone needs to warm and loosen-up their golfing muscles before play. Several exercises are suitable, including the one pictured here — placing a club behind your back and rotating the shoulders and hips. Two others include touching the toes and gently locking the fingers of each hand together and rocking the hands. Make sure you start each exercise gently.

10 HIT A FEW BALLS

Don't make the mistake of slugging away at balls for too long on the practice ground. The main reason you're there is to continue to loosen up your muscles and work on balance and tempo. Don't attempt to hit flat out. Five or 10 three-quarter shots with your wedge, 7-iron and driver are sufficient.

PREPARE FOR YOUR ROUND

11 CHECK YOUR GEAR

Ensure you avoid penalty shots, and even possible disqualification, by carefully examining the equipment in your bag. If playing in a competition, ensure you have no more than 14 clubs, at least a couple of pencils, your opponent's scorecard and a sufficient supply of balls. Incidentally, it's a good idea to mark your balls so you can identify them easily when in play.

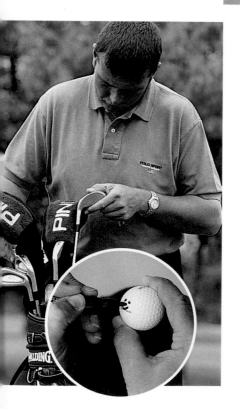

12 SINK A FEW

It's important to build up your confidence and sink a few putts before making your way to the first tee. And the way you do that is by holing from no more than about three feet — missing the hole with longer putts does nothing to help. If you need to gauge the speed of the greens, hit three balls to an area where there is no hole, trying to group them close together.

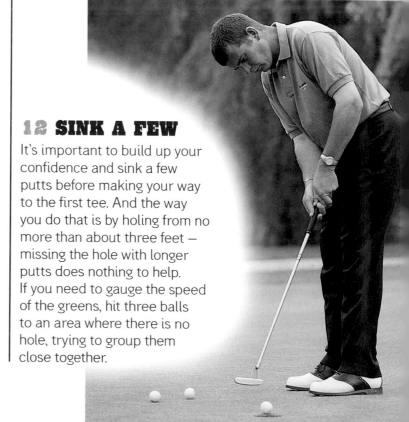

13 SIDEWAYS SOLUTION

If you have difficulty reading borrows from behind the ball, walk up to one side of the hole and determine from there whether you have an uphill or downhill putt. You can then return to the ball knowing whether it will break to the right or left.

14 USE YOUR LOGO

If you decide there is no break at all, it's a good idea to line up the logo on the ball with the flagstick before it is taken out. You then know that the logo is pointing to the dead centre of the hole. If there is a break, pointing the logo to the chosen target line of your putt will help you set up squarely to it.

READ THE GREENS

15 CHECK YOUR SPEED

When studying the line of a putt, remember to look for the way in which the grass grows and lays — known as the nap. It influences how fast the ball rolls. If the grass between the ball and the hole appears shiny, the grain is running away from you and the ball will roll faster than if it appears dull. Another way to spot the way the grass is growing is to look at the area around the hole — the grass will grow across the edge of the cup in the direction that it's lying.

16 NATURAL ANSWER

If you are in doubt about whether there is any break, look beyond the green to determine the natural lie of the land — the putting surface will nearly always mirror it. Remember that greens also usually slope towards any nearby water.

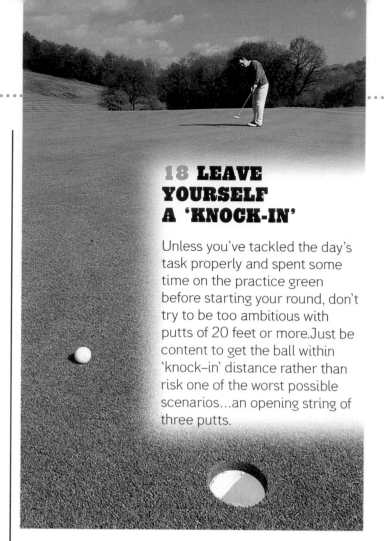

17 OPEN ON A 'HIGH' NOTE

The first tee shot is the most important of the day. Mess it up and you immediately put yourself in a bad mood. A poor round almost certainly looms ahead. So give yourself a break and leave your driver in the bag. Take a club — an iron or an easy-to-use lofted fairway wood — to reduce the risk of disaster. Then make sure you don't spoil your chances by trying to hit too hard.

18 LEAVE YOURSELF A 'KNOCK-IN'

Unless you've tackled the day's task properly and spent some time on the practice green before starting your round, don't try to be too ambitious with putts of 20 feet or more. Just be content to get the ball within 'knock-in' distance rather than risk one of the worst possible scenarios...an opening string of three putts.

GET OFF TO A FLYING START

20 DON'T PUSH YOUR LUCK

If you do happen to find yourself in fairly severe rough early in the round, be realistic and just get the ball back into play with a lofted club. Trying to hit a long club into a green 150 or so yards away usually means you're just one shot away from your next in the rough! You must remember that the rough is the breeding ground of double and triple bogeys.

19 SAFETY FIRST

Early hole bunkers and lakes are more than happy to provide a resting place for balls played by fools. Be realistic and go for the safe part of a green rather than chase glory by taking on a hole cut just behind sand or water. This type of shot should be left until later in the round and only if you're striking the ball really well.

21 CAN YOU TOUCH YOUR TOE?

There is one thing common to every shanked shot. Even though the ball is addressed with the centre of the clubface, by the time it strikes the ball it has moved away from the body, causing a strike from the shank. One of the quickest and best ways to cure this fault is to address the ball opposite the shank and then try and hit it off the toe.

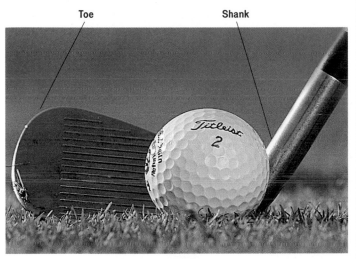

Toe   Shank

Tip about four inches above the knee.

22 DON'T STAND TOO CLOSE

The most obvious reason for shanking is because the ball is addressed too close to the body, causing it to be struck from the shank. A good checkpoint with an iron is to set up to the ball normally and then lower the handle on to the left leg — the tip should touch about four inches above the knee.

STOP SHANKING

Diving in — to trouble.

23 STARTING OUT...

When you take the club back, ensure the head of it remains outside the hands (the same as it was at address). When you get to the top of the backswing you will then come back to the ball on the correct path.

Keep the hands going left — but make sure the clubhead is square.

24 PULL LEFT

Start the downswing by pulling your hands slightly left of the intended line of flight of the ball. The head of the club must again stay outside the hands. This will give you a nicely-flighted shot with plenty of 'hang' time.

Advice from John Cook, coach to England's under-18s team and owner of the Golf Studio at Heathrow Airport.

HOW DO I PLAY THIS?

PROBLEM: The ball has come to rest on a bare lie a few yards from the green. It's a situation that can result in a thinned shot if tackled wrongly.

ANSWER:
Hover the club and attack the ball steeply

The leading edge of a pitching wedge is flat on the ground and is better suited for playing the ball off bare lies.

Bounce on a sand iron lifts the leading edge off the ground, and can easily result in the ball being thinned.

WHICH WEDGE?

A mistake many golfers make with this shot is to go for the sand wedge. This is not the best tool, because its sole design will result in it bouncing off the hard surface and its leading edge skidding into the ball's equator. This will cause a low and out-of-control shot. The club to use is a pitching wedge, which does not have this bounce and can make clean contact with a ball on hardpan lies.

1 HOVER YOUR CLUB ABOVE THE GROUND

It's a good idea to hover the club at address to avoid contact with any stones or twigs and the possibility of moving the ball and incurring a penalty. I position the ball at least halfway back in my stance, keeping the hands ahead of it (looking down, my left hand covers the centre of my left leg). I push my knees towards the target.

2 NOW TAKE A STEEP BACKSWING

The set-up and a slight cocking of the wrists ensure a steep backswing and angle of attack into the ball, which is struck before any contact is made with the ground. I like to keep the backswing restricted, so that I can punch and accelerate the clubhead through the ball, without any breaking of the wrists.

3 ALLOW FOR BACKSPIN

The followthrough is restricted as a result of the solidness of the wrists. The effect of all this, particularly the steep angle of attack, is that the ball runs up the clubface, creating a lot of backspin and a fairly low flight. It will pull up quickly on the second or third bounce on the green so allow for this when deciding where you want the ball to pitch on the green.

PROBLEM: The ball has landed under a tree, wrecking any chance of making a normal swing. It can result in an embarrassing air shot or a thud as your club embeds itself into the top of the ball.

ANSWER: Set the club, look at the ball... and hit

1 STEER IT CLEAR

The first thing you've got to do is set the clubhead in a position that's well clear of trouble.

2 LOOK AT THE BALL...

Leave the club where it is, look down without moving your body and focus on the ball.

3 ...AND NOW HIT IT

Just swing the club down and through the ball. It sounds simple, but it's a little harder to get a good result than it looks. Like most things in golf, the more you practise, the better you'll become.

PROBLEM: The ball has not only come to rest on a severe upslope, but it's also gone and buried itself in the sand. It's a shot that would give Seve palpitations, let alone the rest of us.

ANSWER: Hit down hard and shift a lot of sand

BUNKER BASICS

● The thing to remember with greenside bunkers is that the clubface does not make contact with the ball. It must ride to the pin on a carpet of sand.

● Have a word with your local pro about what type of sand wedge to use. I don't believe most amateurs can handle a club with less than 56 degrees of loft. It also needs plenty of 'bounce' — the design on the wedge's bottom that enables it to cut through the sand

● If the sand is wet, use your pitching wedge rather than the sand iron. The design of your sand wedge will almost certainly cause the club to bounce off the hard sand and skin the ball over the green.

● Judging the actual distance the ball will travel from greenside bunkers is best done by taking into account how far the sand under the ball will fly... in other words, think of the sand and the ball itself as one item.

1 KEEP WEIGHT ON YOUR LEFT

The set-up is crucial. I ensure my knees are pushed forward towards the slope, putting the bulk of my weight on the left side. The ball is central in my stance, and my feet and body are aiming well left of the target. The clubface is wide open.

2 SWING IT LIKE AN AXE

I try to imagine I am chopping wood with an axe — in other words, I am picking up the clubhead very steeply. The weight continues to favour the left side and the knees are kept forwards to promote the steep backswing.

3 JUST GET THE BALL OUT

From my steep backswing, I am now able to come down into the sand about three inches behind the ball. I do not attempt a flowing followthrough — the important thing is to hit down hard and shift a lot of sand, getting the ball up and towards the hole.

TEN WAYS TO CURE THAT SLICE

With these tips, you can rid your game of the dreaded banana shot.

Slice *n.* a result of the club moving across the target line on an out-to-in path with the face in an open position at impact; this action imparts clockwise spin, resulting in the ball curving to the right.

1 EQUIP YOURSELF PROPERLY

Make sure the shafts in your clubs are not too stiff for the speed of your swing. If they are, they will fail to flex sufficiently, leaving the clubface open (pointing right of target) at impact — one of the main causes of the slice. Also make sure there is sufficient loft on your driver. The less loft there is, the higher the sidespin imparted on the ball (and it's usually slice spin for most players). My advice to all but the very good club golfers is to steer clear of drivers with less than 10 degrees of loft. If you are in any doubt about the suitability of the equipment you are playing, seek the advice of your local PGA professional.

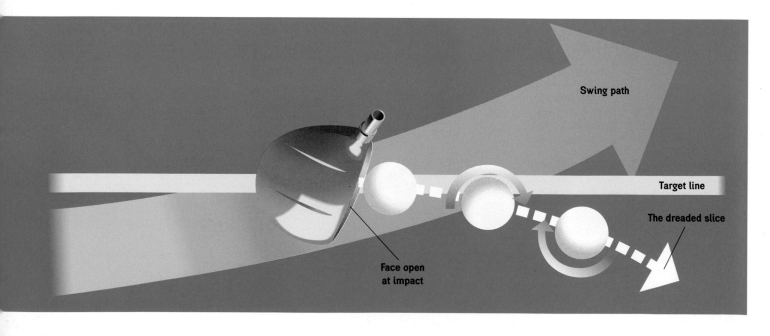

Swing path

Target line

The dreaded slice

Face open at impact

2 WATCH THE FERRULE

How you take the club away at the start of the backswing determines the shape of the swing. Most slicers start the club back using only their hands and arms. This results in an early picking up of the clubhead outside the target line, bending of the left arm and, ultimately, a chopping action back to the ball on an out-to-in path. The club should be taken back smoothly by the hands, arms AND shoulders acting together as one unit. This will lead to the clubhead moving away from the ball on a low path and slightly inside the target line. A good drill for slicers on the practice ground is to watch the path of the clubhead during the first six or eight inches and concentrate on keeping the ferrule slightly inside the target line.

Concentrate on the ferrule slightly inside the target line.

3 POSTURE

It is impossible to achieve the necessary rotation of the shoulders if your spine is too bent and you are generally too hunched at address. This all-too-common posture causes you to sway away from the ball or dip your left shoulder rather than turn it. You also lose height. The outcome is that you have to sway forward to get back to the ball, causing the hands to move too far outside the swingpath and the wrong route (out-to-in) into the ball.

4 TEE IT HIGH

Teeing the ball low with a driver encourages a slicing out-to-in swingpath, whereas a highly-teed ball promotes draw spin. To help eliminate a slice, it's best to tee the ball to at least half as high again as the face of the driver. So ensure you have some long tees in your bag

Checkpoint: A simple, yet very effective, way to establish good posture is to place a club on your right shoulder and bend from the hips until the butt of the handle points at the ball. And that's all there is to it!

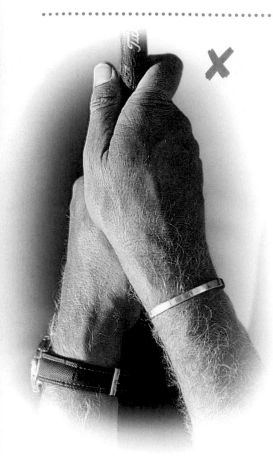

5 POSTURE

Slicing can often be attributed to a bad grip. When you look down on your hands at address, you should be able to see two or three knuckles of your left hand, and the 'Vs' formed by the thumbs and forefingers should point between the chin and right shoulder. If you can see less than a couple of knuckles and your 'Vs' are pointing at your chin, you have the classic slicer's grip. You need to move both hands to the right on the handle.

6 GO TO THE SLOPES

The vast majority of slicers are guilty of starting their downswing with an 'over the top' arms and shoulders motion, which results in them returning the clubhead to the ball on the distance-robbing out-to-in swingpath. An excellent way to get the feeling of swinging to the top and down again on the correct in-to-square-to-in swingpath is to find a slope and take some practise swings and hit balls above the level of the feet. Not only will you get the correct feedback, you'll also most certainly be pleasantly surprised to see the ball ending its flight with a nice little right-to-left draw.

7 SHOULDER ROTATION

If you fail to achieve full rotation of the shoulders in the backswing, your arms separate from your shoulders, causing the left arm to bend and create a very steep swingplane. Your first movement from the top must be to straighten the left arm, usually known as casting... and another very common cause of the slice. Your shoulders have fully rotated when your back is pointing to the target at the top of your backswing.

Checkpoint: A good way to experience the right feeling is to address the ball and then pull your right foot back so that it is almost behind the left. Hitting the ball from this set-up can only be achieved by rotating the shoulders. A good mental picture is of the trick shot where the player hits the ball while on his knees.

8 WRISTS AT THE TOP

The chances of a slice are greatly reduced if you are square to the target at the top of your swing. As far as the wrists are concerned, this has been achieved when the left arm and left wrist are in a straight line. Any cupping of the left wrist inwards can cause a slice. The only way to prevent the dreaded left-to-right ball flight is to make difficult compensations in the downswing so that you can then get the clubhead square at impact.

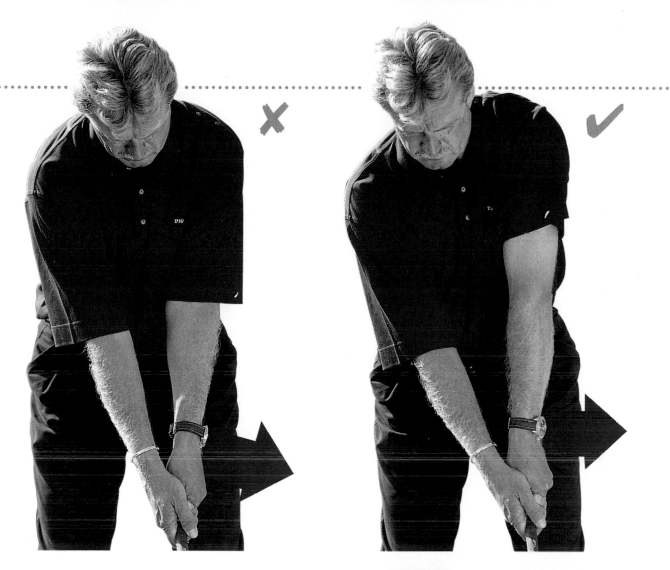

9 ARMS AND SHOULDER CHECK

The face of your watch is a good indicator of where your shoulders are pointing at address. If you are aligned correctly, the face will point at the target. But most habitual slicers line up with their shoulders open (pointing left of target) and the faces of their watches pointing more towards the ground. When I look down at address I also make sure my left arm is slightly further away from my body than my right. This means I will have a strong left side to hit against, rather than a swing where my shoulders spin out of the shot too quickly and cause an out-to-in path through the impact zone.

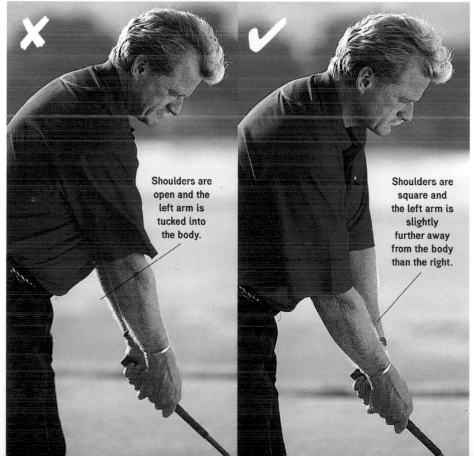

Shoulders are open and the left arm is tucked into the body.

Shoulders are square and the left arm is slightly further away from the body than the right.

Tucking the right arm in on the backswing produces a very flat take-away.

Swing back, and when your left arm is parallel to the ground, the butt of your grip should point to the end of the cane.

10 PLANE TRUTH

Swinging the club on a too flat (or shallow) plane is a very common cause of slicing. The right arm remains too close to the body halfway back and then you have to lift it to complete the backswing, pushing the club outside the desired path. The only way back for the clubhead is on an out-to-in path, cutting across the ball and creating slice spin. A good check on whether you are on the right path is to push a cane (or an old shaft) into the ground parallel to the angle of your shaft at address.

10 CHECKS FOR STRAIGHT HITTING

1
Use the right equipment. Your driver should have at least 10 degrees of loft.

2
Take the club away smoothly and slightly inside the target line.

3
Establish good posture at address.

4
Tee the ball high to promote draw spin.

5
Use a stronger grip with two or three knuckles of your left hand showing.

6
Practise hitting shots off a slope with the ball above your feet.

7
Make a full rotation of the shoulders in the backswing. Your left shoulder should point at the ball before you start the downswing.

8
Check the clubface is square at the top of the backswing.

9
At address make sure your shoulders are square to the target line.

10
Avoid swinging the club on a too shallow plane.

More advice from John Cook,
coach to England's
under–18s team.

THE POWER ISSUE

Go on, hit it 250 yards, and straight down the middle. Actually, you probably don't do it every time, so here we tell you how to add accurate power to your drives.

One of the requirements of a powerful strike is to maintain your height from start to finish. This is best achieved by holding your chin off the chest at address and keeping it off until after impact. Other essentials are that knees should be flexed (rather than bent), to help create leverage during the downswing and that your arms are tension-free.

The right shoulder should be relaxed and, because the right hand is below the left on the handle, will automatically be lower than the left. Don't exaggerate this — it's natural.

A good thought to adopt at address is to maintain your height throughout the swing.

The arms should hang down naturally without any tension.

The right hand should be parallel to the left and the 'V' formed between the thumb and forefinger should point about halfway between the chin and shoulder.

When you look down at your left hand, you should be able to see two knuckles.

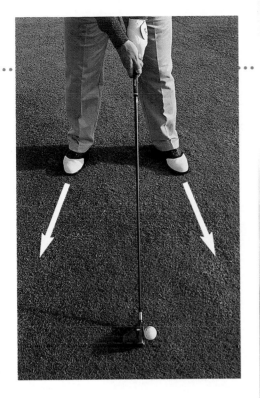

To create maximum power, you stand in such a way that your turn during the backswing is resisted by the inside of the right leg. This is done by standing with your right foot splayed out at about three minutes past the hour. Your left foot is splayed slightly more (about six minutes to the hour) so you can turn right through the shot to a full followthrough.

Try to keep your back reasonably straight. Bend from just above the navel rather than the waist.

The chin is held off the chest to allow a full shoulder turn and help to maintain height throughout the swing.

If you lowered the driver onto your left leg, it should rest about two or three inches above the knee.

Flex your knees rather than bend them. Too much bending will result in a loss of power.

POWER POINTS

1 SMOOTH MOVE
Clubhead speed, and therefore distance, is virtually impossible to achieve without a tension-free swing. Relax by hovering your driver just above the ground at address.

2 HEAD BEHIND BALL
Concentrating on keeping your head behind the ball at impact allows the lower half of the body to move into the shot first, transferring weight to the left foot and contributing to a powerful strike.

3 LOW AND SLOW
A useful thought to promote the necessary wide swing arc for distance is to start the clubhead back low and slow. It also helps promote good tempo.

3 UP AND AWAY
With the ball positioned just inside the left heel at address for the drive, the left hip and shoulder should be higher than the right. This will help promote the feeling of hitting the ball on the upswing.

There's no point in hitting the ball 300 yards if you can't keep it straight.

5 LEFT TO RIGHT
Many players never reach their distance potential because they don't rotate their arms in the throughswing. A good thought is of trying to touch the left forearm with the right. You won't achieve it, but it's a good image.

6 BE ACCURATE
The further you hit the ball the more accurate you have to be. In a fairway of 40-yard width, a 300-yard drive has to be a third more accurate to stay on the short grass.

Teeing the ball at this height encourages the desired upward hit halfway up the clubface.

TOP OF SWING

A powerful and full backswing is determined by how far the body turns, rather than by how far the clubhead travels, and is achieved when the left shoulder points at the ball and the back faces the target. This, together with resistance from the right leg, results in a full and powerful coiling of the body.

Turn until your left shoulder points at the ball and your back is facing the target.

Because the chin was held off the chest at address, the left shoulder can now slot nicely under it and the eyes kept focussed on the ball.

The right knee remains flexed (above, left) to resist the body turn and create the coil effect necessary for distance. Buckling of the right leg (above right) leads to lateral swaying and triggers all sorts of problems.

HAVE A BALL

A wide backswing, with the hands well away from the shoulder at the top, is essential. A great way of achieving this is to try this drill. You must ensure there is enough room for a soccer ball to lodge between the two.

POWER MYTHS

You've heard it all before at the clubhouse bar: "I hit the ball miles off the tee, but I just couldn't putt." We don't think it's actually 'miles', so decided to ask the professional and some members of March Golf Club how far they hit off the tee... and then asked them to prove it.

The professional, 26-year-old Phil Dimmock, expected to hit his driver a maximum of 275 yards, with an average of about 270. No kidding, he hit all ten balls within ten yards of each other between 265 and 275 yards out.

Wally Crawley, a senior who played off single figures for many years and is now a handful off 14, put his figure at 225 with his driver. He was about 10 yards off, although one 'out of the middle' passed the 235-yard mark.

John Wells, handicap 22, predicted that he would hit about 200 yards with his 3-wood (he doesn't use a driver). In fact, he averaged just three yards short of his prediction. He had a best of 210 yards.

Ian Philpott, a newcomer to the game with a handicap of 28, did not expect to hit further than about 180 yards with his driver. He was right. A few of his balls reached 180, but his average was five yards less.

Robert Roe, who is 14 and plays off 23, said that he would probably reach about 210 yards using his driver. He did make the distance with a couple of balls, but had to settle for an average of 199 yards.

HALFWAY DOWN

Power in the downswing comes through uncoiling the left side which, in turn, pulls the club down to create leverage. This movement also clears the left side so that when the club reaches the hitting area there's plenty of room for it to travel on through towards the target before it heads inside again to the followthrough.

The chin is kept high throughout the downswing to allow the right shoulder to pass under and into the followthrough.

Separating the left shoulder from the chin automatically slots the club into a very powerful position.

The uncoiling of the left side causes the right elbow to tuck correctly into the side.

When the club is brought down correctly the toe should be facing the sky at this point.

The left hip is clearing out of the way to create plenty of room for the club to travel through towards the target.

Separation of the left shoulder away from the chin at the start of the downswing stops any possibility of 'coming over the top' and into the ball on an out-to-in path. It also helps to keep the head behind the ball at impact.

PROVE IT...

A great drill to feel the power created by the uncoiling left side is to hook a clubhead behind a tree and pull. You will soon discover you can create more leverage, and therefore power, from your left shoulder and hip than you can from your right side.

POWER PLAY

There are no 'ideal specs' that make a big hitter, and size really doesn't matter — it's just not the most important issue, for powerful strikers come in all shapes and sizes.

Take a look at these different-sized tour stars and discover some of the secrets of how they obtain their prolific yardages off the tee.

TIGER WOODS

Tiger stands very tall at address and maintains his height throughout. He achieves a perfect top-of-swing position (with his left shoulder pointing at the ball) and then uncoils his left side with fantastic, but controlled, speed. He's also able to release the clubhead fast enough with his hands and arms to cope with the high speed of his uncoiling action. The last point is crucial. The release must work in unison with the speed of the left side.

IAN WOOSMAN

One of the reasons why the little Welsh star (he is 5ft 4in) manages to hit the ball so far is because he has built a classic swing and has worked hard to establish great strength in his back and arms. This allows him to turn his back completely to the target at the top of his backswing and then move through from the left side to achieve terrific clubhead speed through impact. He continues to turn through until his stomach faces the target.

JOHN DALY

At the top of his swing Daly looks to be out of control. This is not so. You will see that his shoulder has turned no further than to point at the ball. The reason he's able to let the clubhead fall well beyond parallel is his suppleness. Being able to point his left arm virtually straight up to the sky at this point gives him time to create tremendous leverage and speed during the downswing. Few people are supple enough to achieve this.

IMPACT AND FOLLOWTHROUGH

Instead of sliding your weight to the left side, which normally creates a push shot to the right, it's best to feel that you are turning your left side out of the way at the same time as you're transferring your weight to the front foot.

The head has stayed behind the ball through impact.

The left shoulder continues to separate away from the chin.

The back of the left hand faces the target at impact.

Note how the legs are working together at this point.

The left leg begins to turn to the left as the club goes through.

The outside of the right foot begins to come off the ground as the weight moves towards the left.

JUST IMAGINE...

Using a rugby ball to illustrate the point, a pass where the ball goes to the right means in golf terms that the rotation of the hands and arms has not been completed. The result will be a push to the right or a left to right slice flightpath.

Over-rotation will lead to the ball being struck with a slightly closed clubface and will result in a shot pulled to the left or one that travels from right to left.

Correct release of the clubhead at impact is achieved through the rotation of the hands and arms, as opposed to a flicking action. Using the rugby ball, the correct action would result in it being passed accurately to someone standing square to you. Note how you have to turn your left side to make this possible — exactly the same applies with the golf swing.

AND FINALLY...

The proof of a powerful and balanced action can be found at the very end of the swing.

A perfectly-balanced followthrough sees the stomach facing the target and the weight on the outside of the left heel. A player should be able to lift his right leg off the ground without falling over.

SHORT GAME SHOTS

Turn three shots into two around the greens and watch your handicap tumble.

One of the most risky (and duffed) shots for amateurs is the high lob into a green from about 50 yards. Unless a lot of height is crucial, the best bet to achieve control from this range is the punch shot with a pitching wedge. The ball is played a little further back in the stance, with the club gripped down the handle and the knees leaning towards the target. The arms travel no further than waist height in the backswing and followthrough and remain connected with the body throughout. A good checkpoint is that the toe of the club should be pointing to the sky at completion of the shot.

The arms travel no further than waist height and stay connected with the body throughout.

Play the ball a little back in the stance and punch with a wedge.

The toe of the club should finish pointing to the sky.

DON'T CHUNK YOUR CHIPS

You will never hit consistently solid chip shots if you allow your wrists to dominate the stroke. Players who get flicky at impact run the risk of thinning it clean through the green or chunking it a few inches. Try the check drill on the right before every chip shot to prevent that wristy action and the disastrous results. Also, focus particularly on your right wrist as you play the shot. Its angle at impact should be the same as it was at address. Only that way can you guarantee solid contact.

CHECK DRILL
Don't give yourself a body blow

Grip a club well down the shaft and play a practice chip. You're breaking your wrists if the handle strikes you.

The handle of the club will stay well away from you if your wrist action is correct.

If you flick at the ball, the right palm faces the sky.

SHOULD IT STAY OR SHOULD IT GO?

It seems trivial, but even the decision to remove the flag or leave it in when you are just off the green can have a significant effect on your score. If you face a slippery downhill putt from the fringe it is wise to keep the flag in. The hole is not only easier to see, but the pin can stop your ball in its tracks if it's running too fast. If the shot is uphill you can afford to be more aggressive. In this situation, take the flag out.

Work on retaining the angle of the right wrist.

The flag stays in for downhill shots...

... but take it out when you're playing uphill.

SANDY SOLUTION

A nightmare shot for nearly all club golfers is having to play to a green from a sandy lie just behind a bunker. It normally results in a half-hearted flick... and the ball in the bunker. The fact is that what you are facing is nothing more than a bunker shot. So take your sand wedge, stand with your shoulders pointing to the left of the pin, hit behind the ball and let the sole of the club work for you by splashing it over the bunker on a cushion of sand to the green. The margin for error is much greater than if the ball had landed a few inches further back and on harder ground. Then you would have to select the pitching wedge and make a very accurate and clean contact with the ball.

Set up with your body aiming left of the target, as you normally would in the sand, and play the splash shot.

Just a few inches further back and you are faced with a completely different shot. Play it with a pitching wedge.

HOLLOW VICTORY

Although they may be within a few yards of the pin, grassy hollows can spell disaster if the ball is sitting well down. To avoid fluffing the shot only a few inches, you must try to avoid getting a lot of grass between clubface and ball. And the way to do this is to use a sand or lob wedge, then position the ball back in your stance. Now stand open (pointing to about 11 o'clock) and then use plenty of wrist action to pick the club up steeply and hit down positively through impact.

Avoid trapping grass between your club and the ball.

Hinge your wrists to create a steep backswing, and then hit down positively and through.

MORE BIRDIES, FEWER BOGEYS

Don't try a career best with a wood. Instead, lay up short with an iron.

How you can start marking birdies on your scorecard — without having to spend a fortune on lessons or gear. It's simple, and you don't have to be a single-figure handicapper.

TAKE THE SAFE PLAY

Here we have a par–5 which requires plenty of thought. It's time to apply the '75 per cent rule'. With water guarding the green about 220 yards away, the chances of landing the ball on the putting surface are less than 75 per cent... so the sensible thing to do is take an iron and play up short of the water and about 80 yards from the pin.

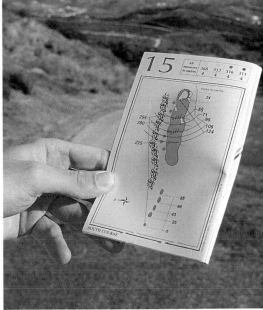

PITCH IT STIFF

A pitch over the water and a single putt will result in a birdie. But, remember, it is vital to keep practising this area of the game. One of the main reasons for Tiger Woods' vast improvement over the past couple of seasons is his countless hours of effort hitting high and low shots into the pin from within 100 yards.

Practise more shots from 100 yards in.

USE YOUR HEAD OFF THE TEE

From this elevated tee, you probably feel like thumping your driver downhill to the green about 360 yards away. But a close inspection reveals there is big trouble on both sides of a very narrow fairway. So play a long iron to the short stuff and you stand a chance of making a birdie three. If you try a smash with the big stick, you may have to hack the ball out of bushes or thick rough, and risk a double-bogey — or worse.

COURSE MANAGEMENT

The very mention of the subject has been known to instantly cure severe cases of insomnia. Yet, like it or not, it is one of the most important aspects of the game, and often the only difference between a good player and a bad one.

TOP TIP CHECKLIST

1 DISTANCE
Make sure you know the distances you can hit with each club. Most poor players don't have any clear idea of this — and it's one of the reasons they're poor players!

2 PRACTICE
Your first shot can dictate your mood for the whole round — so get to the course in time and make sure you give yourself a chance to hit a few practice shots.

3 THE WIND
It is much easier in windy conditions to allow for the wind to take your ball left or right, rather than trying to fight it. Leave that to Tour players, who have the experience.

A straight-faced club will allow the ball to run out to the hole.

A straight-faced club will allow the ball to run out to the hole.

CHIP LIKE YOU PUTT

Most players are more happy putting than chipping. So when it comes to shots around the green, do as the Professionals do and think of your bag as containing 14 different lofted putters. Using your normal putting technique and grip, take the lofted clubs when you have little green to work with and the straighter-faced ones when you want to run the ball low to the hole.

CHIP TIP

When chipping, concentrate on keeping your hands ahead of the ball, both at address and through the stroke.

Beware tee markers that point directly to bunkers.

LINING UP FOR TROUBLE

Players often miss the target because they have lined themselves up with badly-aligned teeing grounds or tee markers. Take a look at this picture and you will see that the player has done just that — and will almost certainly strike the ball to the left.

Step back and look at the target.

The feet, hips and shoulders are now perfectly parallel to the target line. A birdie putt is probably the next shot... rather than one from the difficult bunkers to the left of the green.

Much better. This shot's heading for the heart of the green.

TAKE AIM, THEN FIRE

The correct way to take aim is to look at the target from behind and then pick a spot about two feet behind the ball and in a straight line to it. Now carefully line yourself with your feet, hips and shoulders parallel to the spot you have selected.

BIRDIE CHECKLIST
Think about the game to save shots

1 HIT THROUGH
No matter what type of shot you're faced with, remember to concentrate on hitting through that ball rather than at it.

2 SPINNING
Remember that although high-spinning balls stop quickly on greens, they also spin further off line when clubhead contact is not correct.

3 SCRUB UP
Shots are easily lost because of shiny, slippery grips. Keep them tacky by scrubbing regularly with washing-up liquid and warm water.

SPLASH THE TEE FROM THE SAND

Bunker success is about having the confidence to hit the ball to the pin on a carpet of sand. A good way to get a good feel for the shot is to draw a two-inch circle in the sand, place a tee peg in the middle and then splash the sand and tee peg to the pin. This will rid you of any negative thoughts about thinning the ball.

Draw a circle in the sand and hit a tee peg from it.

Hole six or seven medium putts on the trot — then go and do it on the course.

PUTTING PATIENCE

All your good work to the green will be in vain if you fail to convert those medium-distance putts from about 15 feet. One of the best ways to knock shots off your scores is to practise this important area of the game whenever you can. A good exercise that can improve things is to line up six or seven balls and continue until you have sunk them all in successive strikes — and remember to be patient!

CHECKLIST TO KNOCK OFF SHOTS

1 TENSION
Bad shots are often the result of gripping the club too tightly, tensing the arm muscles and swinging jerkily. Stay loose!

2 LOOK UP
Most short putts are missed because the player looks up too soon. Wait to hear the ball drop in the hole first.

3 DISTANCE
Always play within yourself — you should never swing at more than 80 per cent of your maximum speed. Make sure you take plenty of club.

4 PUTTS
Let downhill putts 'die' in the hole and hit uphill putts into the back of it. Simple advice, but often ignored by bad performers on the green.

5 SHADES
Are you a poor reader of greens? Cutting glare by wearing sunglasses may be a solution for you. With them, some players say they see the contours more easily.

BE A BETTER PUTTER

Hole more long putts and impress your friends. That's the guarantee as we take you to the green for a set of putting routines.

1 ONE HAND ONLY

The game: Putt a set number of balls to a target with one hand only on the club and then try using the other hand. Now putt with two hands on the club, and you'll find that the stroke feels really solid.

How it helps: It gives you a good feel for the head of the putter and helps keep it square through impact. It also prevents the wrists breaking down at impact.

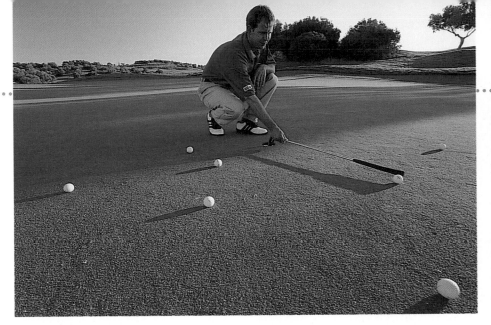

2 THE SWEEP

The game: Scatter several balls round the perimeter of the practice green and see how many of them you can get within a sweep of your putter from the hole. A sweep is where you place the head of your putter in the hole and then twist it round a full 360 degrees.

How it helps: You'll become better at long putts and eliminate those annoying three shotters.

2 A GAME OF BOWLS

The game: Follows the same rules as crown green bowls. Use a tennis ball as the jack and each player takes it in turn to putt four balls to it. The winner is the player who scores the most points over a set number of 'ends' or the first to reach a set number of points.

How it helps: Introduces fun and a variety of putts into your practise.

3 LEAPFROG

The game: Take it in turn to try to putt a yard beyond your opponent's previous effort. Decide who goes first and how many balls for each player. The game is lost if your ball fails to reach the last ball played, strikes it or rolls beyond one yard.

How it helps: You get a feel for the pace of putts. It also helps you get the ball past the hole more often.

6 GAME ON

The game: Use one ball each and have a 'match' over a set number of holes on the practice green. Whichever player wins the hole picks the spot from where the next putt is taken.

How it helps: Introduces a competitive edge and helps you handle pressure on the greens, particularly if you have a couple of quid on the outcome!

5 PUTT TO THE SHAFT

The game: Place a club on the ground, decide how many balls each player will use for each game and then take it in turns to putt to the shaft of the club. You only score a point if your ball finishes within a putter's length of the shaft. Striking it or rolling the ball past means you're out.

How it helps: Improves your feel for distance and pace.

7 THE PLANT

The game: Similar to a 'plant' in snooker. Place a ball about three inches from the hole and try to sink it by striking another ball from two or three yards into the back of it. If you putt the ball correctly it will send the target ball into the hole.

How it helps: It trains you to be positive with your strokes around the hole.

8 MASTER THE SLOPES

The game: Find yourself a green with a good slope. Now mark with a tee peg the spot where you think you should aim so the ball dies in the hole... and see if you were right!

How it helps: Takes the fear out of slopes when you encounter them for real on the course.

9 RIGHT LENGTH DOES THE BUSINESS

Many players do recognise the importance of selecting the right type of putter. It is, after all, the most used club in the bag – but few realise just how vital it is to get the correct length of shaft. The overall objective when putting is to try and create a simple pendulum action, which cannot be achieved when, as with most players, the putter is too long. The correct length will encourage the correct posture by tilting forward predominantly from the waist and the hips. The eyes will be directly over the ball and the arms will hang vertically down from the shoulder sockets. With this posture, the face will feel as though it is perfectly parallel to the ground (Colin Montgomerie is a wonderful example) and the left forearm and shaft of the club form virtually a straight line. You can now create a natural pendulum motion, allowing the arms and putter to swing straight back and through along the target line. To complete the recipe for success, grip the handle predominantly through the palm of the left hand to encourage an arched left wrist and avoid manipulation of the putter face through the stroke.

Arms hang naturally from shoulders.

Eyes above ball. Face parallel to ground.

The left forearm and shaft form straight line. The left wrist is arched.

Eyes well inside ball, face not parallel.

Poor posture.

There is an angle between arms and club shaft.

The toe of the putter is raised.

The perfect fit for a putter. You now have the correct posture to create a simple pendulum action. The eyes are positioned directly over the ball with the face being parallel to the ground. Also the arms hang naturally from the shoulders.

Putter is too long. It makes correct alignment almost impossible. The path of the stroke becomes too much of an arc as the shoulders turn rather than slightly tilt. The stroke will be too wristy and the clubhead will overtake the hands, causing poor contact.

A natural pendulum putting stroke involves starting the club back with a movement of the shoulders. The triangle formed between them and the hands remains intact.

Retaining the triangle shape will allow the putter face to strike the ball while travelling slightly upward, thus imparting overspin to help produce roll.

A DOZEN PUTTING TIPS FOR INSTANT SUCCESS

1 NO DOUBTS
Don't take too long over your putt once you have decided on the line and pace. Freezing over the ball and letting doubt creep into your mind are two of the most common causes of missed putts.

2 GET CLOSE
Be realistic in your ambitions. So don't go for and expect to hole long putts — trying this will only lead to frustration and disappointment. Getting nice and close to the hole is good enough from 20 feet and more.

3 HEAD DOWN
There are a great many tips to help you keep your head down during the stroke. One of the most successful of these tips is to concentrate on keeping your left shoulder low through the stroke.

4 ON THE BALL
Don't look away in disgust when your ball goes beyond the hole. Keeping your eye on exactly where the ball has gone will provide you with valuable information for making an accurate return putt.

5 INSPECTION
Inspecting closely how the grain of the grass lies can help you judge the pace of your putts accurately. You must expect to hit the ball harder if the grain is against you.

6 IMAGINATION
Using imaginary holes for uphill and downhill putts can help with accurate pace. For instance, on uphill putts you should aim to sink the ball in a hole behind the real one. The reverse is the case when going for downhill ones.

7 CHECK THE ANGLE
One of the most effective ways of preventing the wrists breaking down through impact is to concentrate on maintaining the angle formed at address between right hand and wrist.

8 DON'T JERK
Poor putters often ruin their chances of success by jerking the putter head away from the ball. Hovering the clubhead above the ground at address helps to solve the problem.

9 RIGHT SPOT
An easy way of establishing exactly where the ball should be positioned is to adopt your address and drop the ball from the bridge of your nose. The spot where it lands is the correct place.

10 NO FEAR
If you are frightened of charging the ball past the hole on downhill putts, try hitting it off the toe of your club. In this case, the ball will not go as far as when it is hit off the centre.

11 TOPSPIN
Move the ball slightly forward in your stance when faced with slow or bumpy greens. Hitting it slightly on the upswing will promote topspin and help it roll better.

12 FAST SWING
The head of the putter should NEVER decelerate at impact with the ball. You should reduce the length of your backswing when practising to help you achieve an accelerating stroke through the ball.

THE BEST BUNKER TIPS EVER

We hope you never have to use them. But just in case, here's how to get out of every bunker you are likely to come across.

60 YARDS OUT

With 60 yards to go to the pin, this shot appears to less experienced players as harder than it really is. In fact, it's not much different from a normal iron shot from a fairway. Rather than a ball–then–turf contact, it's simply a case of ball then sand. From this distance, it is played with the pitching wedge.

The ball is positioned just forward of centre.

Grip a little tighter than normal to help prevent unnecessary wrist hinge.

Don't wriggle your feet down into the sand, as it will lower the base of your swing and may lead to you striking the sand before the ball — the desired contact for a greenside bunker, but not from a fairway trap. Create a stance that is firm enough to offer just enough support and stability to make a balanced swing.

Weight is evenly distributed, and the feet, hips and shoulders are all set parallel to the target line.

Normal distance   Stand closer

Stand nearer to the ball to encourage a slightly steeper angle of attack and a clean contact. A good way of gauging the distance is to position the grip one hand's width from your thigh (above left) rather than normal where the fingers are outstretched (above right).

USING A WOOD

Put most amateurs in a fairway bunker and tell them to go for a green about 180 yards away with a fairway wood, and you would think you had asked them to take on The Old Course at St Andrews armed only with a table tennis bat and a football. But, provided you have nothing short of a perfect lie and are satisfied that the loft on the clubface is more than enough for the ball to clear the lip of the bunker, there is no reason why they shouldn't take it on. Although the objective is to hit the ball cleanly, set up with your feet, hips and shoulders aiming slightly left of

target to allow you to get more bounce off the sand if you do happen to make contact with it. Grip about halfway down the handle for better control and a cleaner strike, and position the ball back in your stance about two or three inches behind your normal set-up position for this club.

As far as the swing is concerned, the emphasis is on upper-body movement. It's important to take the club back a little more on the inside than normal and feel that the left arm is travelling across the chest. This will enable the club to attack the ball more from the inside, to create a shallower

swingpath and avoid taking a deep divot of sand. On the downswing, you should feel as though you are turning your right shoulder hard through impact. This encourages the upper body to turn through the shot and pull the arms and club powerfully through, rather than attempting a weak flick with the hands, as most amateurs do. Finally, concentrate throughout the shot on keeping the head still to avoid excessive lateral movement.

One greenside bunker, same lie, but — because of a change in pin positions — two different shots are needed. The first pin is only four or five yards beyond the lip and the shot needs plenty of stop on the ball when it lands. The second has 20 yards of green to play with. This is how they can be played.

Aim shoulders, hips and feet to the left of the target.

Open the clubface so it aims just right of the target.

Contact with the sand should be two inches behind the ball.

Hold the clubface open through impact and restrict the followthrough.

For this type of shot open the face of the club and cut across the ball.

THE STOPPER

Slicing across the ball with the clubface of my sand iron nice and open will help get the stop I need on this awkward little shot.

I achieve this by aligning my feet, hips and shoulders to the left of the pin but opening the clubface so it aims just to the right of target. With the hands positioned just behind the ball, all I now have to do is simply swing the clubhead along the line of my feet, hips and shoulders and contact the sand two inches behind the ball, holding the clubface open through impact and restricting the follow-through. With the ball positioned opposite the left heel, the bounce built into the sole of the club and the out-to-in swingpath will prevent it digging too deeply into the sand. A good feel to have for this shot is as though the left arm moves away from the body in the backswing.

Make sure that when you are in a hazard to be very careful what you touch. You are allowed to move anything artificial (termed an obstruction) but not anything natural (termed a loose impediment). In the example pictured right, you may therefore move the empty golf ball packet but not the leaves and twigs. If in moving the packet the ball itself happens to move, it should be replaced without penalty. The best advice is: if you think there is a possibility it may move, mark it just in case.

Align the shoulders, hips and feet square to the target.

The clubface should also point at the flag.

Take a shorter backswing and hit an inch behind the ball.

Turn your hips and shoulders off to the left. This will pull the arms across the body and on to a full finish.

Sit the face of the club square and the ball will roll out once it has hit the green.

THE ROLLER

The object of this shot is to land the ball on the green and let it roll to the pin. This is done by positioning the ball just to the left of centre in the stance, aligning my feet, hips, shoulders AND clubface square to the target, taking a shorter backswing (almost three-quarter) and hitting about an inch behind the ball. I ensure I don't quit on the shot by turning my hips and shoulders off to the left of target, which pulls the arms across the body and on to a full finish position. Unlike opening the face to produce backspin, this type of approach will prove invaluable when you are playing a course where the greens are large and many of the bunker shots could be over bigger than average expanses of green.

WHICH SAND IRON?

HAVE YOU GOT THE SOLE FOR IT?

Few amateurs give much thought as to the type of sand iron to use. Sand irons come in various shapes and sizes, but the two key features are the amount of clubface loft and the bounce in the sole. Clubface loft speaks for itself, but the question of bounce is not always understood. It is the distance that the bottom of the sole extends below the leading edge of the clubface. Place a club with plenty of bounce squarely on a table and you will see the leading edge of the club sits off the surface. The average amount of loft on 'off the shelf' sand irons is about 56

degrees with 11 degrees of bounce. Bounce stops the clubhead burying itself too deeply into the sand, so light, fluffy sand is best dealt with by a club with plenty of bounce (13 or 14 degrees); hard or wet sand is best played with clubs of about five degrees. A club with lots of bounce is not suited for chip shots off short grass around the green, particularly if the ground is hard. The sole will invariably bounce off the ground and cause the leading edge to skid into the centre of the ball and cause a nasty thin — that's why lob wedges possess hardly any bounce at all.

Here you can clearly see the bounce built into the sole.

The degree of bounce.

The normal amount of loft on a sand iron is 56 degrees.

Sit a club with plenty of bounce on a table and the leading edge will be above the surface.

AND IF YOU CONTINUE TO STRUGGLE IN BUNKERS...

One of the strangest looking clubs to arrive on the scene in recent years is The Alien sand wedge, which was unashamedly aimed at those who have virtually given up hope of ever hitting a ball out of sand with conventional equipment. "We guarantee you'll get out of any sand trap with your first swing," said the adverts, together with three simple things you had to do: Just square up to the target, keep your hands ahead of the ball, and hit it fat. Many golfers shelled out the asking price of about £70 in those

days and suddenly discovered that their enjoyment on the course didn't have to end every time the ball finished in a bunker. Having found an Alien gathering dust in a dark corner of our equipment cupboard, we decided to see if the magic still works. Two golfers, both honest enough to admit their sand play was not always at its best, were handed the club and told what they were supposed to do. Velma Amps (handicap 31) was as near to being overjoyed as possible on a cold day and wet golf course. "It's the first

time I've hit so many consecutive shots out of a bunker. It's simple to use and I really like it — in fact, I think I will buy one," she said. Derek Rowlett (handicap 10) also had no trouble at all making it work from a greenside trap, but, being an experienced player, spotted the club's only weakness. "It certainly gets the ball up and out, although I don't think it's a club for delicacy and pinpoint accuracy," he said.
● The Alien is available through Genesis Management Group (0161 7283522) at £59.99.

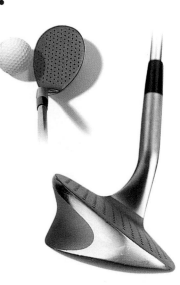

Avoid lifting your body during the swing.

Concentrate about 80 percent of your weight on the left foot.

BALL BELOW FEET

This is a much easier shot to play than it appears at first sight. An extra wide stance is essential to allow you to get the clubhead down to the ball. Aim slightly left of target, with about 60 percent of your weight on the left foot. The ball should be positioned in the centre of the stance, and a sharp wrist break is necessary to achieve a steep angle of attack. Play the shot mainly with your arms and wrists, and avoid lifting your body during the swing.

STEEP FACE

The ball needs to be positioned just inside the left heel, with your feet, knees, hips and shoulders all aligned to the left of the target. The club itself should be aimed at, or even a little right of, the target and be laid open so flat that you can stand a glass of wine on it! Using a sharp wrist break, swing the club along the line of your body to cut the ball up high. The weight should slightly favour the left side, and it's important to keep 'sitting down' on the shot to allow a shallow divot to be taken to provide extra height and distance as required.

PLUGGED AND UPHILL LIE

It's important to get your knees leaning into the slope, with about 80 percent of your weight concentrated on the left foot. The ball is played just inside the right heel, and the hands at address are opposite the left thigh to create the necessary steep angle of attack. With the clubface square to the target and your body aiming a little left, take the club back with wrist break and hit down one inch behind the ball, making sure you keep the hands ahead of it at impact.

WET OR HARDPAN?

The ball is positioned back in the stance so that the hands are forward of it at address and can 'pinch' it off the sand. The weight favours the left foot (about 70 percent) and the wrists are broken early in the swing. Aim to make contact with the sand about half-an-inch behind the ball — any further back and you risk the club bouncing off the surface and striking the ball too cleanly.

DOWNHILL

An extra wide stance is needed to allow you to put your body at right angles to the slope. About 80 percent of your weight needs to be on the left foot, and an open clubface and open stance are used to enable you to cut across the ball from outside to in and get it up quickly. The ball at address should be positioned between the centre of your stance and the back foot. The shot is then played using a sharp wrist break, keeping the weight on the left side so that you feel as though you are swinging down the slope. Avoid scooping the ball up.

SAVE SHOTS BEFORE YOU PLAY

We all know that rushing to the 1st tee is no way to prepare for a game so why do we do it? It won't be just your mate you upset. Your game won't be too clever, either. Do yourself a favour: warm up. Tiger Woods has his pre-round routine, so what makes you think you don't need one?

Panic adds up to a 1st hole nightmare.

Sadly it's a familiar story — had a late night, forgot to set the alarm for that early tee time, skip breakfast, break the speed limit on the way to the course and change into your spikes in the car as your trolley rolls across the tarmac. Sprinting to the 1st tee gets you hot and bothered but it's no way to warm up. Lame excuses don't convince your mate that you aren't a twit. You scramble through your pockets, searching for that lucky tee and ball. Every weekend you perform this circus act and top your first drive or slice it out of bounds. An eight at the first or a scorecard blob is the norm. When will you learn? We could all take a lesson from the boy scouts and their motto: Be prepared...

You must warm up. Try this quick exercise. Place a club across your shoulders and rotate back and through as if you're making a golf swing. Repeat five or six times.

Start the round with a long iron instead of your driver. Concentrate on hitting the fairway with your first shot.

You'll be left with a longer second shot but be realistic. Play a mid-iron and leave yourself an easy approach.

You should still walk off the green with a bogey or maybe even a par. Use the first few holes to steadily build your confidence. Then you can start going for your shots

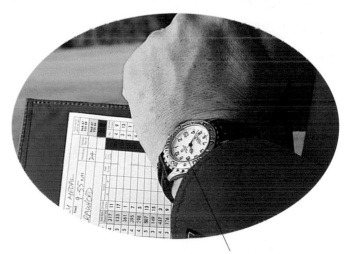

There's no substitute for arriving half an hour before you tee off, and then making proper use of your time. Find out how on the next pages.

YOUR 30-MINUTE WARM-UP ROUTINE

Don't simply hit one ball after another. You must have a routine that loosens your muscles and clears your mind of negative thoughts. Make time to get your game off to a flying start.

Half an hour before teeing off is not the time to start working on your swing. Instead, it's a time for finding good rhythm and tempo.

30 MINUTES TO GO

Warm up by holding two clubs together and making several easy practice swings.

25 MINUTES TO GO

Most of your preparation will be on the practice range. But don't take balls and hit them aimlessly. Choose three clubs — a wedge, 7-iron and driver — and work through them. Hit half a dozen balls with the wedge, then do the same with your 7-iron and finally the driver. Work your way back down with the 7-iron and finish warming up with the wedge.

10 MINUTES TO GO

Throw balls in a bunker and work on your feel for the shot.

5 MINUTES TO GO

Hit 10 three-foot putts uphill. The idea is to build up your confidence. Remember that the pace of greens on the course is usually quicker than that on the practice putting green so remember to take this into account.

TIME TO TEE OFF

Your body should be warmed up and your mind clear of doubts. Now make a slow and controlled swing and watch that first drive of the day sail down the middle of the fairway.

Don't try this at home! See next page to find out how Tiger Woods warms up

HOW THE WORLD'S No1 GOLFER GETS HIMSELF READY TO PLAY

MINUTES 10-15
5-iron
Five straight shots, approx 190 yards.
Five draws
Five fades.

He may be the coolest golfer on God's Earth but he's also one of the most dedicated and professional. Just watching him warm up will convince you of that. At the Open Championship earlier this year, we observed and recorded his every move on the range and were hugely impressed at how meticulous he was. Every day he followed the same routine as if he were pre-programmed, hitting the same number of balls with the same clubs to the same targets. Occasionally, just to prove he is a human being after all, he shared a joke with Steve Williams (caddy) or Butch Harmon (coach) before returning to the very serious business of loosening up and scaring the living daylights out of all the other players on the range who couldn't help taking a peek at the man they knew they had to beat. Apart from the professional approach, perhaps the most important lesson to learn from Tiger's warm-up is that it is precisely that – a warm-up. At no point did Tiger consult with Harmon on technique and it was clear the coach was present purely for support and to offer an encouraging word or two. So as we take you through Tiger's session, bear in mind that the sole reason for his doing it is to establish a repetitive rhythm for the day, not alter his swing.

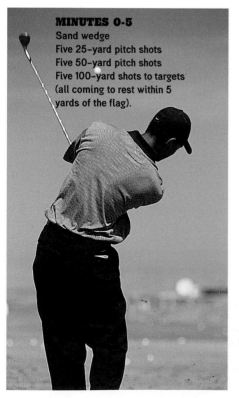

MINUTES 0-5
Sand wedge
Five 25-yard pitch shots
Five 50-yard pitch shots
Five 100-yard shots to targets (all coming to rest within 5 yards of the flag).

MINUTES 5-10
8-iron Five straight shots to target approx 150 yards away – all fly on exactly the same line and trajectory.
Five draws to same target – all on exactly the same line and trajectory.
Five fades, same everything.

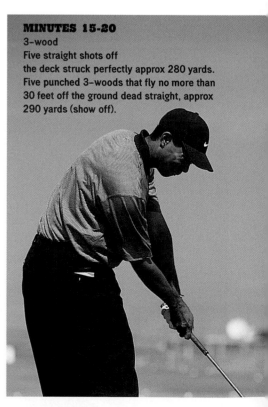

MINUTES 15-20
3-wood
Five straight shots off the deck struck perfectly approx 280 yards.
Five punched 3-woods that fly no more than 30 feet off the ground dead straight, approx 290 yards (show off).

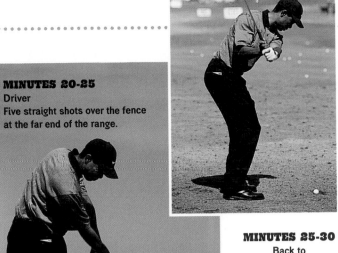

MINUTES 20-25
Driver
Five straight shots over the fence at the far end of the range.

MINUTES 25-30
Back to
sand wedge
A couple of shots with the 5-iron and 8-iron again before finishing with a few sand wedges.

TIGER'S DISTANCE vs YOURS

(Carry and roll, average strikes)

THE CLUBS	TIGER HITS	MR AVERAGE'S HITS		
		LOW H'CAP	MID H'CAP	HIGH H'CAP
Driver	290 yards	240	220	200
3-wood	260	225	205	180
2-iron	225	210	NA	NA
3-iron	215	195	180	170
4-iron	205	185	170	160
5-iron	190	175	160	150
6-iron	180	165	150	140
7-iron	170	155	140	130
8-iron	160	145	130	120
9-iron	150	135	120	110
PW	135	125	110	100
SW	115	105	90	75
LW	100–105			
Average Hits	185 yards	170	160	140

● Mr Average's average distances could be either plus or minus ten yards on the above figures.

TIGER THEN MOVES TO THE SHORT GAME AREA

MINUTES 30-35
Bunker play
To practise his sand play effectively Tiger stuck a rake in the practice bunker to recreate the height of the bunker faces out on the course.

MINUTES 35-40
Pitching Pitch shots from about 70 yards short of the green to three different holes. Each checking to within five or six feet.

MINUTES 40-45
Chipping Chip shots from 20–30 yards to a single hole.

MINUTES 45-50
Transported by minibus to practice putting green behind grandstand.

MINUTES 50-55
Putting It is noticeable that Tiger hits most of his putts from 15-20 feet. It soon dawns on us that that is the distance he expects to hit all of his approach shots to. Unlike amateur golfers, who should hit a lot of uphill

3-4 footers, Tiger virtually ignores this length putt.

MINUTES 55-60
Composing himself on the 1st tee Tiger arrives with plenty of time to spare. There is no rush, and he has a minute or two to say hello to Ivor Robson (the starter) and to his playing companion. He receives his pin location chart and hits a few more putts on the tee. When Tiger is announced he gives a brief wave to the crowd, before focussing once again on where he wants to position his tee shot and then belting his ball with a long iron down the middle into that perfect spot from which to attack the flag. GAME ON!

QUICK FIXES

Improve your chances of a good score by following these quick tips.

HANDY DRILL TO STOP THINS

One of the most common problems I see with club golfers trying to play pitch shots onto the green is that they try to help the ball into the air with their right hand. This has exactly the opposite effect...a thinned shot. If you are familiar with this story, a good drill is to hit shots off a good lie or a low tee peg with your left hand only, trying to keep it ahead of the ball through impact. This drill will help you understand that this shot calls for a fairly steep angle of attack to achieve good contact and get some spin.

TIME TO BELT UP

Elbows splaying or separating during the swing is a common fault and causes inconsistency. Here is a sure-fire cure: Loop a belt (or a tie, piece of string etc) so that it gently holds your elbows together at address. Now swing the club, making sure you keep the belt taut from start to finish. This drill will help you feel the proper position of the elbows which, in turn, will ensure the clubhead remains square to the target through impact.

DON'T SPOIL A GOOD THING

Golf is quite hard enough to play without us having to make it even more so. That's why you should follow the example of the great tour professionals and ALWAYS use a peg off the tee instead of just dropping it onto the turf. Teeing your ball up even just a little results in less resistance between ball and club, therefore reducing the risk of a wayward shot. So why turn down the chance of a perfect lie?

ALL TOGETHER NOW...

An excellent practice drill to rid yourself of lateral sway and to improve balance and tempo is to swing back and through with your feet together. Any swaying or balance problems will result in you toppling or, if you've REALLY got a problem, falling over! The secret of success is to concentrate on making a nice smooth swing with an upper body turn rather than a sideways movement of the body. Take this turning motion and balance to the course and watch your scores tumble.

MAKE POSITIVE PUTTS

Don't make the common mistake of putting unnecessary pressure on yourself by trying to hole long putts when practising before your round. Missing them will fill you with negative thoughts rather than positive ones. Instead, concentrate on the quality of strike and distance control to instil confidence. An excellent method is to use two headcovers about four feet apart and simply putt balls between the two. If you want to use a hole, be content to smack a few balls into it from no more than three feet.

Before your round concentrate on quality of strike and distance control. Putt between two headcovers placed four feet apart instead of at a hole — this will help to remove any negative thoughts if you miss.

POSTURE CAN SAVE SHOTS

Thousands of words have been written on the importance of good posture at address. A simple and good mental image to adopt is that of a soccer goalkeeper waiting for a penalty kick to be taken against him. Weight is concentrated on the balls of the feet, legs are slightly flexed, and the spine is not hunched. The overall feeling is athletic and lively rather than one of tension.

FOCUS ON MAKING A SMOOTH GETAWAY

Many players whip the club away from the ball so quickly that they rob themselves of any chance of a swing with a nice tempo. One way to ensure a smooth start is to concentrate on seeing the clubhead for the first six or eight inches of its path. But don't make the mistake of allowing your head to move back with the club. Follow its path with your eyes only. Now concentrate on maintaining a smooth rhythm throughout the swing.

PINPOINT YOUR SPOT FOR BETTER CHIP SHOTS

Most poor chippers aim in the general direction of where they want the ball to go rather than at an exact spot where they want it to land. Watch the tour pros and you'll see them preparing thoroughly for a shot. They actually build up a mental picture of the shot . Then, by making several practice swings, they allow their 'mental data banks' to produce feel for the exact length of swing needed. You should try doing the same thing.

SHADY SOLUTION

Sunny days can be used to check whether you are guilty of the common errors of body sway, excessive head movement, and loss of height during your swing. Stand with the sun behind you and take up an address position where the shadow of your head covers a tee peg. Any movement of the shadow during your swing will soon become evident. Incidentally, although lateral movement of the body and loss of height (dipping) should be avoided, many of the top teaching professionals say it is perfectly okay for the head to move back a little during the backswing — as long as it.stays behind the ball at impact.

Place a tee peg in the ground, as illustrated above, and use it to check excessive head movement during your swing. Try to avoid too much movement, although a little is not disastrous.

LOOK FOR THE MARKER

Falling to the temptation of seeing the ball drop into the hole on short putts, many players allow their heads to come up through impact. This drags the shoulders and rest of the body to the left when the ball is struck, causing it to miss the cup on the left. A good practice drill to prevent this is to place a marker under the ball and continue to look and focus on it until well after the ball has gone (hopefully into the hole). You can then use the mental image of the marker as a useful aid when you have to make short putts on the course.

TRY THE PARALLEL BAR DRILL

When it comes to clubhead path and alignment, the humble piece of 2 x 2–inch timber is still as effective as any practice aid. By placing a length of it just beyond the ball and parallel to the hole, you can immediately discover if the head of your putter is square to the target line at address and whether it travels along the correct line back and through or across it. As far as indoor practice is concerned, a skirting board offers exactly the same checkpoints.

CONSISTENT TEMPO

A couple of soft headcovers can help establish consistent tempo and judge distances. Place the covers the width of your stance apart and, starting with the putter in the middle, make ten strokes forward and ten back, just touching each cover. Then close your eyes and continue to try to make light contact with the covers. Once you have 'cracked' this distance, keep moving the covers further apart (up to a maximum of about three feet) and repeat the exercise.

HOLING THOSE FAST DOWNHILL PUTTS

Many amateurs experience real problems with downhill putts because they focus on the hole when mentally fixing the pace. And that often leads to the ball charging past the cup and into three-putt territory. The best way to prevent this is to putt to an imaginary hole in front of the actual one, allowing the slope to add enough natural pace to take the ball over it and into the real cup.

On tricky downhill putts focus on a spot in front of the hole and imagine putting to it. This will help you to judge the correct pace of the real thing.

KEEP YOUR KNEES STILL

Look at all the leading tour professionals and you will notice a complete absence of leg and body movement during their putting strokes. An excellent way to help you achieve the same action is to concentrate on keeping your knees absolutely still during your stroke. It really works.

CHIP THE BALL OUT OF THE SAND

If your ball lands in a greenside bunker with very little lip, it's often worth considering playing a chip–type shot rather than a full explosion, particularly if there's water behind the green. Position the ball back in your stance with the hands ahead of it and then make the shot almost entirely with your arms. There should be virtually no movement of the legs or turn of the shoulders. You should also try to avoid cocking the wrists.

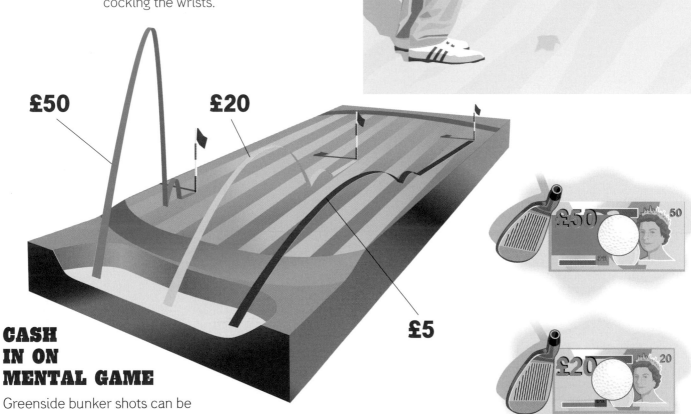

£50

£20

£5

CASH IN ON MENTAL GAME

Greenside bunker shots can be controlled by the amount of sand you take as well as by adjusting the length of swing. The image of various banknotes is a useful mental thought to help gauge just how much sand should be taken for various distances. If, for instance, the ball is close to the pin, imagine it is sitting in the middle of a £50 note and aim to strike the sand at the front of the note and to remove it completely from the bunker. The image of the smaller £20 note should be used for a shot to a pin a little further away (therefore taking a little less sand) and the £5 note for a flag position a good distance away.

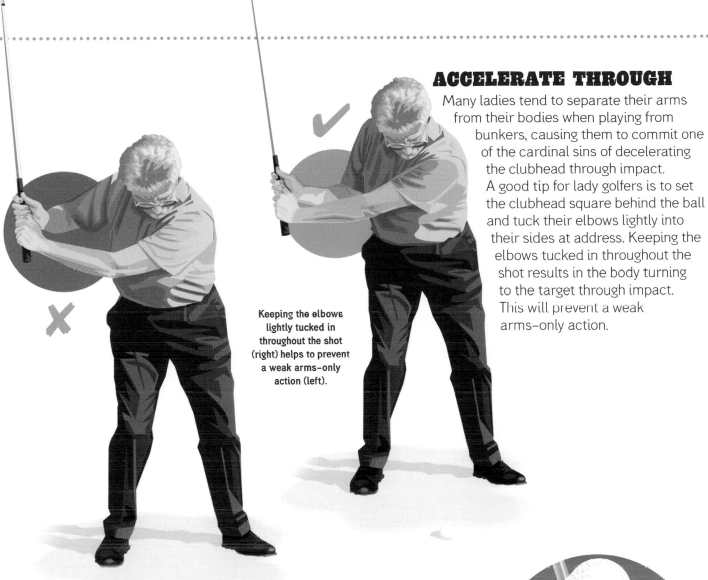

ACCELERATE THROUGH

Many ladies tend to separate their arms from their bodies when playing from bunkers, causing them to commit one of the cardinal sins of decelerating the clubhead through impact.

A good tip for lady golfers is to set the clubhead square behind the ball and tuck their elbows lightly into their sides at address. Keeping the elbows tucked in throughout the shot results in the body turning to the target through impact. This will prevent a weak arms-only action.

Keeping the elbows lightly tucked in throughout the shot (right) helps to prevent a weak arms-only action (left).

THE TEE DRILL

An excellent drill to encourage you to slide the club under the ball and explode it out on a cushion of sand is to sit it on a tee and push it right down into the sand. Then try and take a long and shallow 'divot' and clip the tee out with the leading edge of the clubface. You can go a long way towards achieving success by remembering to keep your left arm moving throughout the shot.

BUYER'S GUIDE

On the pages following, we list things to watch for when you go to the golfing shop, so you can get the best equipment possible.

We start with a look at the clubs a golfer carries. You can carry up to 14 clubs in your bag — a driver, 3 and 5-woods, nine irons (3 to sand wedge), putter, and maybe a lob wedge. But you don't always have to carry the full load. Why not carry just the clubs you need?

COST CUTTER:
One of these could save you a small fortune in golf balls. Don't be ashamed to carry it. Think of the long-term savings!

IRON OUT FAIRWAY PROBLEMS
Forget the 3 and 4-irons. It's difficult to hit them consistently, especially off a tight fairway lie. Instead of hoping to hit a powerful 3-iron into the heart of a green (let's face it, you're not going to do that very often) opt for the 7-wood, or even a 5 or 6-iron and a chip. Irons that are oversized and cavity-backed will give huge consistency advantages.

THE HIGH HANDICAPPER

CLUB CHECKLIST
- Oversized 3 and 5-woods
- 7-wood
- Oversized 5-iron to pitching wedge
- Big flange sand wedge
- Large headed lob wedge
- Putter

WHERE'S THE DRIVER?
High handicappers get in more trouble with the big dog than any other club in the bag. So don't carry one. Opt instead for the consistency of an oversize 3-wood, which has a shorter shaft and slightly more loft. The 5-wood is an alternative to the 3-iron. A 7-wood gives consistency off the fairway and is great on long par-3s.

CONSISTENT AND ACCURATE
Bunkers are a nightmare for higher handicappers. If you struggle in the sand, then a wedge which comes as part of a full set can often compound your problems. In that case, a specialist wedge with a large flange is a must. They look awful but work incredibly well. They will flop a ball on to the green from difficult lies. You can forget finesse, but you'll be a better player for using one. A lob wedge is optional. As a high handicapper you will miss greens on approach shots, whether it be left, right or short. The lob wedge could be a crucial shot-saver around the cut stuff.

THE MID HANDICAPPER

CLUB CHECKLIST
- Titanium driver
- Sole weighted 3, 5 and 7-woods
- Cavity-backed 5-iron to pitching wedge
- Specialist sand wedge
- Large headed lob wedge
- Putter

HELP FROM THE SOLE
Although you may have a consistent swing most of the time, a bit of help getting the ball in the air is always welcome. A new breed of drivers and fairway woods, with heavy metal weights in the sole, will help you to get the ball in the air quicker. Most mid-handicappers will find that 10.5 or 11.5 degrees of loft will be about right for the driver, and if you can afford it, the large head properties of titanium would be a huge benefit.

THE SPECIALS
A specialist 57-degree wedge can be one of the most useful clubs in the bag. Pick a good one like this and you'll have a club with a slightly rounded leading edge that makes bunker play much easier. They are also excellent for chip and runs around the green. The lob wedge can be a lifesaver. The added loft is perfect for shots when playing into protected greens, where flags are tight to the front of the green.

DON'T CARRY LONG IRONS OUT OF HABIT
You'll notice the 3 and 4-irons have been left out, and a 7-wood placed in the bag instead. You might not get the same penetrating ball flight from a 7-wood, but consistency is the key.

THE LOW HANDICAPPER

CLUB CHECKLIST
- Titanium driver
- Compact fairway wood
- Special 2-iron
- Semi-blade 3 to 9-iron
- Three wedges
- Putter

GO FOR POWER
Better golfers want a powerful wood, preferably titanium, which gives a strong trajectory. There is nothing worse for a single-figure golfer than hitting a club that balloons the ball into the air, losing valuable yards. Added to this is a compact steel fairway wood that will come into its own, especially on par-5s when there may be a chance of hitting the green in two.

GO FOR LOOKS AND FEEL
Better players are not interested in game improvement technology. They are looking for two things — looks and feel — and being able to control shots is their key objective. Compact heads allow this to happen. Unlike the high handicapper, they want to be able to hit a fade or draw to order.

CRAFT YOUR SHOTS
Carry a specialist pitching, sand and lob club. Very often forged heads will be a preference because they complement a soft golf ball and impart more spin on the ball. We have also included a copper lob wedge. A different head material will produce a different feel and this will add to the confidence of the better golfer.

TEE SHOT ALTERNATIVES
The 2-iron is a great club in the right hands. It works superbly when you need to hit a low tee shot through the wind, it's also a real benefit for long par-4s and 5s. For the good player this is a guaranteed 200-yards plus in any conditions.

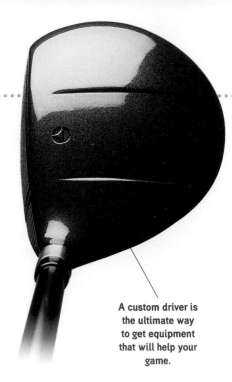

SEVEN QUESTIONS TO ASK BEFORE YOU BUY A NEW DRIVER

1 What's my starting point?

How much do you want to spend? It can be anything from £30 to more than £300. Remember that paying more doesn't necessarily mean you will get the best driver for you.

2 How do I decide which loft I want?

As a general rule, better players go for lower lofts, as they have less trouble getting the ball in the air. If you are a beginner or tend to hit the ball very low, the more loft the better. Go for around 12 degrees.

3 What about shaft flex?

This is the most important part of any driver. The shaft, mixed with your swing, determines whether you hook, fade, draw or slice the ball. But every golfer going shopping has a problem — there are no industry standards on flexes, so one maker's 'regular' can be different from another's. This is why there is a real need to try a demo club.

4 What about a titanium clubhead?

Titanium has one major benefit over steel. It also has a fairly obvious drawback. The good thing about it is that it is lighter and stronger than steel. This means the manufacturers can make bigger clubheads with no weight gains, which improves the golfer's confidence standing over the ball. Contrary to popular opinion, you won't notice any great distance advantages over steel. The minus point to titanium is that it costs more than steel, but in recent years prices have started to fall.

5 Are there any benefits in having a club custom-fitted?

Yes — there is nothing better for your confidence than using a club that is tailored for you. Although custom-fitting is more common when buying a set of irons, a lot of manufacturers are realising that it is equally important with drivers. Shaft, grip, how the club sits on the ground (upright, flat, anti-fade, anti-hook) are all considerations when you go for a custom-fitting process.

6 Should I buy an offset driver?

If you hit sliced tee shots then 'offset' could solve quite a few short-term problems. Offset drivers are designed as instant problem-solvers for the average golfer who hits a left to right shot (that's if you're right-handed). The only issue you might have with offset drivers is the look, which can verge on the ugly. But do you want results or a nice-looking club?

7 Why do drivers have heavy metal inserts in the sole?

By placing weight in the head of the club, designers can move the centre of gravity, which will help or hinder the ease of use of the club. In drivers it's more common to see weights in the back of the head (to aid a higher ball flight) or towards the heel (to help square the face at impact). Sole weighting is more common in fairway woods.

A custom driver is the ultimate way to get equipment that will help your game.

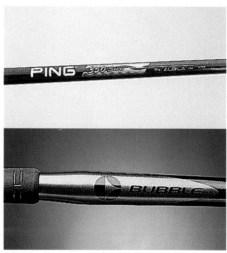

The shaft is the most important part of a driver. There are many types to try.

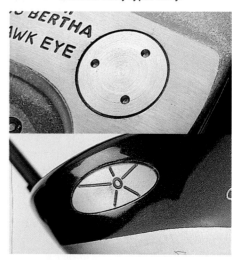

Metal weights move the centre of gravity.

Classic blade putter.

QUESTIONS YOU NEED TO ASK TO CHOOSE YOUR IDEAL PUTTER

1 Which putters are right for my own putting stroke?

There are two basic styles of putting stroke. Here's how to check which style you use, so your club follows your style rather than the other way around... If you stand with your weight biased slightly on your left foot, you will 'rap' the putt. You tend to pick up the putter more steeply on the way back, instead of keeping it low to the ground. You'll accelerate through, and stop your followthrough quite quickly. What you need is a bladed putter. But if you take your club back low to the ground, and hit the ball when you're stroke is slightly on the upswing, then you're 'rolling' your putt (the putt rolls further as a result). You should use a mallet putter.

Roll with a mallet.

Rap with a blade.

2 Does wrist action come into it?

If you keep your wrists stiff, you'll find you pull the club through the stroke, rather than trying to hit at the ball. You'll benefit from a mallet putter. But if your wrists are flexing, use a bladed putter.

3 Does the way I stand dictate which putter I should use?

If you like putting with the ball towards your front foot, you will tend to hit the ball on the upswing, which will favour a mallet putter. If the ball is placed in the centre of your stance then a blade or Ping-type putter with some loft is better.

Heel and toe weighted putter.

4 What about my height or arm length?

Because every individual is such a mixed bag of genes, it's more useful to think about your putter as being an extension of your arms. A club pro or shop will have a selection of shaft lengths to try. Longer putter shafts can be cut down to suit your arm length.

5 I'm a nervous putter. Can I solve it with equipment?

If you're finding it hard to relax on the green, a broomhandle putter, (named after it's extra-long shaft) can provide more stability.

6 Can I get a putting advantage over course conditions or the weather?

If you putt during the winter in the UK, greens are mostly longer and damper, and therefore slower. Having something that is made of a material that makes the ball go off the blade fairly quickly is good. Ping putters made of steel or copper are good for that. But if you're used to playing on fast greens, it could be a good idea to buy one of those putters with a softer insert so that the ball doesn't spring off the face so violently.

Soft inserts are good for quick greens. The ball doesn't spring off the face so violently.

7 Will a selection of putters give me an advantage?

If you find you lose confidence with one putter, it may help to change to another of a similar type.

Full mallet putter.

FIVE QUESTIONS TO ASK BEFORE YOU BUY A SET OF IRONS

1 What is the difference between a cavity backed iron compared to a blade?

Neither head hits the ball further than the other, that comes from the quality of the strike. The blade is not as forgiving as a cavity-backed club, but in general the heads will be more compact, and the golfer will feel more when they hit the ball. Bladed irons have less offset in the heads. Offset is designed to help the golfer square the face easier and better players don't need it, so a limited amount of offset is confined to the long irons. Cavity backed irons have the weight positioned around the edge of the club so that they give the maximum amount of forgiveness. Game improvers down to single–figure players will get the best from cavity backed irons and single–figure handicappers to professionals will use blades.

2 Is there a benefit to forged heads?

Forged heads are softer than cast. This means you get a different type of feel when you hit the ball. Forged steel sends more back to the golfer's hands than cast steel. Although more cavity backed forged clubs are now available for the mid handicap players, it's primarily the better golfers who will benefit from the softer heads. An important point to consider is that forged heads mark easily. Any knock can tarnish the look of the club in the long term.

Extra weight in the sole helps get the ball in the air easily.

If you want a soft feel go for a club with a forged head.

As a general rule, graphite is lighter than steel... but dearer.

3 What's the difference between graphite and steel shafts?

Graphite has come a long way, but so has steel. The benefit of having graphite shafts is the weight saving. Because they are lighter, you can create greater swing speed with no extra effort. The strong swinger of the golf club won't really benefit from this, but the lady, junior or senior player will gain. Creating more speed means you will gain a few extra yards.

4 Does the thickness of the grips matter?

Yes. This is overlooked by the vast majority of weekend golfers. If you think about it, how can someone with small hands get the same out of an iron as someone with very large hands? As a general rule, when you fold your left hand around the grip (that's if you're a right-handed golfer) the longest finger should just touch the palm of your hand. If it digs into the palm, then the grip is too small. If the finger doesn't touch, then the grip is too fat. A grip which is too thin can promote a hook, as the hands become too active in the swing. Grips which are too thick promote a fade.

5 How do heavy metal inserts in clubheads help?

By placing heavy metal plugs in iron heads you are moving the centre of gravity to improve its playing characteristics. You will normally find heavy metal plugs in the sole of irons. This moves the centre of gravity lower in the head, which allows the ball to get up in the air quicker. Moving weight from the heel/toe of the club is also beneficial. Most club golfers pull short irons into greens (they miss it left), therefore weight is placed in the heel to help keep the face square at impact. Likewise with long irons, the natural shot for most golfers is a fade, so by putting more weight in the toe, it helps keep the face square, rather than open it at impact with the ball.

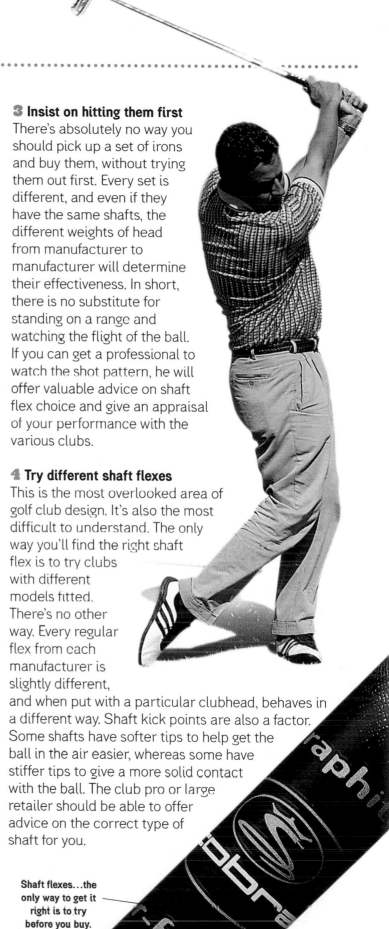

FOUR WAYS TO PICK YOUR NEW IRONS

SHOPPING LIST
TAYLOR MADE FIRESOLE TOUR £579
LYNX PARALLAX ... £549
TITLEIST ... £590 ... £13
... PLUS £599

1 Make a shortlist and try them all

The choice of new irons is massive… and daunting. In order to make the right decision you must narrow the list down so that it fits in with what you want in terms of type of club (oversize, traditional, blade etc) and price. It's then important to try all the clubs. Forget what anyone else thinks, what feels right to you is the most important thing. Don't buy a set because they are on a 'limited special offer' without hitting them. It could be your biggest waste of money ever.

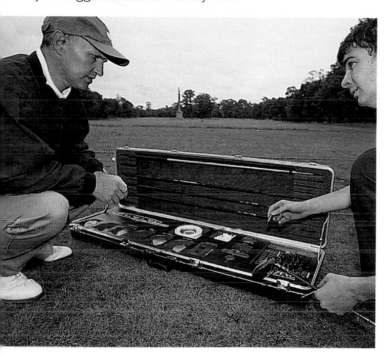

There's nothing like a set of custom irons for helping you to try your best. They make you feel good, too!

2 Have them custom fitted

This could be a major confidence booster. Getting the lie angle and shaft length set for your style of swing is a plus point, without a doubt. It's not a difficult proposition either, as of the major manufacturers offer a custom fitting service. You may not be able to go into a pro shop and walk out with a custom fitted set (these are normally ordered by your pro/retailer from the manufacturer) but the wait is certainly worthwhile. Standing over a ball with a club you know is just right for you, is a great benefit.

3 Insist on hitting them first

There's absolutely no way you should pick up a set of irons and buy them, without trying them out first. Every set is different, and even if they have the same shafts, the different weights of head from manufacturer to manufacturer will determine their effectiveness. In short, there is no substitute for standing on a range and watching the flight of the ball. If you can get a professional to watch the shot pattern, he will offer valuable advice on shaft flex choice and give an appraisal of your performance with the various clubs.

4 Try different shaft flexes

This is the most overlooked area of golf club design. It's also the most difficult to understand. The only way you'll find the right shaft flex is to try clubs with different models fitted. There's no other way. Every regular flex from each manufacturer is slightly different, and when put with a particular clubhead, behaves in a different way. Shaft kick points are also a factor. Some shafts have softer tips to help get the ball in the air easier, whereas some have stiffer tips to give a more solid contact with the ball. The club pro or large retailer should be able to offer advice on the correct type of shaft for you.

Shaft flexes…the only way to get it right is to try before you buy.

SECRETS OF THE BEST GOLF BALLS

Before golf ball technology went through the roof, picking the right ball for your game was not that demanding a task. If it was greater distance and durability you looked for, a solid two-piece ball was ideal. If superior feel and a higher spin rate were top of your wish list a wound three-piece would fit the bill. It was that easy. Things are more complex nowadays, of course. There are no longer just two types of ball construction — now there are five!

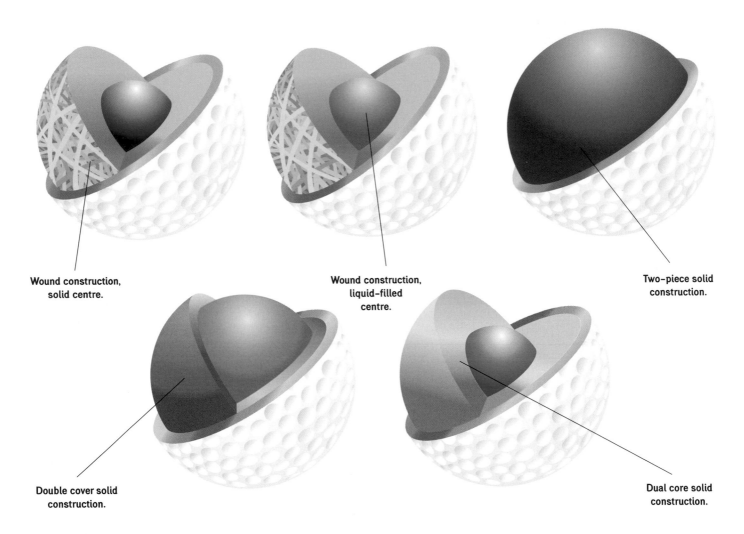

Wound construction, solid centre.

Wound construction, liquid-filled centre.

Two-piece solid construction.

Double cover solid construction.

Dual core solid construction.

Every golf ball can be classified into one of the categories shown above. The old perception that solid balls feel hard and go a long way, while wound balls spin more and feel soft no longer holds true. Some solid construction balls have been designed in such a way as to give high spin rates and relatively soft feel, whereas some wound balls have such low driver spin they are as long as many two-piece distance balls. Not at all confusing then. So how do you decide which ball is best suited to your game? Really, there is only one method that will guarantee you end up with the right one; try as many as you can!

WHAT MAKES A GOOD GOLF BAG?

Not all golf bags are made the same. Some, like the Sun Mountain Ascent SLX (pictured here), are so well made that they could last you a lifetime. Others are less well designed — they may feel cumbersome, cause you a lot of discomfort and could fall to pieces after a year or two's gentle use. So how do you avoid letting go of £100 or more for a piece of trash? Easy. Next time you're eyeing up a potential replacement ask yourself this simple question: can it match the features shown here?

A dual strap will distribute the bag's weight over both your shoulders, making it more comfortable. Important if rounds drag on and on.

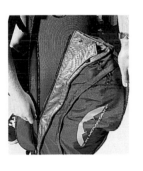

A detachable clothing pocket will lighten a bag if you don't think you'll need extra clothing.

If you tend to pack for all eventualities you'll need a lot of space. A clothing pocket and four others is probably the minimum.

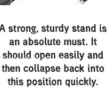

A strong, sturdy stand is an absolute must. It should open easily and then collapse back into this position quickly.

A light bag — this one weighs just 5lb — means you will come off the 18th green still able to walk. Heavier bags will punish your back and legs.

Extra padding where the bag is in contact with your body will make it even easier to carry.

THE BEST GOLF SHOES SCORE WELL IN SIX AREAS

If you don't want to come home with soggy feet, walk five miles in absolute agony or worse, look frightfully untrendy, then you'd better choose the right golf shoes. A comfortable fit is probably the first thing to look for, followed closely by style, waterproofing, breathability, traction and price. Finding a pair which scores highly in all six areas can be a tough proposition, but a low score in any one of them could lead to disaster. So before you go out and buy a new pair of golf shoes, make sure that the shoes are the best possible.

Mizuno's T-Zoid Wave comes complete with a free accessory pack which includes a bag for each shoe. It's a nice little extra which club golfers will appreciate.

A reinforced heel area which has plenty of padding is essential if you are looking for long-term comfort.

Special plate adds to this shoe's stability and helps to absorb more shocks while you walk.

Full grain leather uppers with a waterproof guarantee. These are a must for all-weather golf.

A solid sole unit will give comfort and cushioning. Just what you need on a long walk!

Look for a sole with a specially-designed pattern to offer the best possible grip during the golf swing and while you walk the fairways.

WEAR GOOD GLOVES FOR BETTER GOLF PLAY

If you think your glove isn't really that important try playing your best golf wearing a crusty old rag that's been lurking at the bottom of your bag since the 1970s. You'll get no grip and consequently hold the club much tighter. A flurry of slices will probably follow and the resulting score will cause you acute embarrassment for months to come. It will also feel uncomfortable. A spanking new pair of tight-fitting gloves is what you need. With this you'll look, feel, and play considerably better. Gloves are not too expensive either – £15 is the right sort of price range for a top of the range pair.

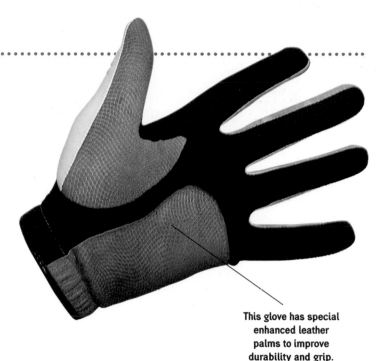

This glove has special enhanced leather palms to improve durability and grip.

Lycra along the finger gussets and knuckles provides a consistent, customised and comfortable fit.

Digital Fiber-Sof microfibre in the back, palm and fingers offers additional grip and increased durability with a soft, leather-like feel.

Graphite-enhanced leather provides the ultimate in durability while giving great grip.

ACKNOWLEDGEMENTS

We wish to thank the following individuals and organizations for their help and assistance and for supplying material in their collections:

Golf Professionals and Instructors
Gareth Benson
John Cook
Alastair Davies
Phil Dimmock
Jason Froggatt
Andy Lamb
Mark Reed
Alison Sheard
Derek Simpson
Paul Simpson
Martyn Vaughan
Alan White
Simon Wordsworth

Golf Clubs and Organizations
British Airways
Cambridgeshire Moat House Hotel Golf Club
Celtic Manor Resort, Newport
Golf Studio, Heathrow Airport
Hart Common Golf Club, Bolton
Hunstanton Golf Club
Kingsbarns, Scotland
La Cala Resort, Spain
La Manga Resort, Spain
Lanark Golf Club
March Golf Club
Montecastillo Resort, Spain
National Golf Club, Turkey
Sheringham Golf Club
Tat Beach Club Golf Resort, Turkey
West Wilts Golf Club

Photographers and illustrators
Bob Atkins
Terry Begg
Graham Gaches
Angus Murray